Green Elephants

How internal service providers can deliver amazing value

Simon Chapleau

ISBN-13: 978-1492776376
ISBN-10: 1492776378

Dedication

To my wife and daughter, the Agents in my life.

Table of content

Introduction

How I became obsessed with internal service providers

When I finished university I was given the opportunity of a lifetime: work for IBM in their software lab. Never mind that I studied chemistry and the labs I was used to contained beakers and Erlenmeyers, not high-performance computers.

Little did I know I would actually be working for the support organization at the lab: their internal service provider. I quickly came to realize that there were two different types of people working at the lab: those who brought in money and those who wasted it. Well, at least according to those who brought money in.

Programmers were considered the earners. They created products that were sold with tremendous profit margins. They were making a difference in a variety of fields like weather prediction, molecular modelling and epidemiology research.

And then there was me. Supporting the application that contained all of the code (what techies call configuration management and version control system). It was a critical application. When the application failed, programmers were not able to get their work done, and clients couldn't be supported. But as the saying goes: "It's not because you are necessary that you are important."

Internal service providers as cost centres

One of the many perks of working for IBM was that they had great access to educational programs. In fact, due to a glitch in their system I was able to complete two master's degrees at the same time: one an MBA and the other in project management (I guess they never thought someone would be dumb enough to try it).

During my MBA program I saw what it took to make companies profitable and how back office costs needed to be squashed like bugs. IT, HR, finance, legal, logistics, customer service; these departments needed to be managed aggressively and every drop of productivity extracted from their overpaid personnel.

At least, this is the perception that all my business books and professors gave me. Internal service departments were cost centres. By their very definition they don't create value and were a cost of doing business, like government taxation. Centralization and outsourcing were the big trends at that time to reduce costs as much as possible.

Working for a cost centre myself I became very ashamed of being such a leech. How could I be handicapping this company I loved by being part of a cost centre? So I decided to become a consultant and jump on the revenue side of the equation.

Internal service providers don't want new clients

After IBM I went to work for another powerhouse in the IT world: Gartner. I was very excited to work for one of the most renowned IT management consulting firms in the world.

As I began working with a variety of clients (mostly internal IT departments), it became very clear that most of my MBA training was useless. Not because it wasn't accurate or realistic. But because most of what I learned had one basic assumption; companies want to increase customers and increase their revenues. But that's not the case with internal service providers.

What do you do when your budget is fixed, no matter how many customers you have? That's right, you don't want any new customers. And that's the situation for most internal service providers. That's also why most business strategies fail in an ISP environment: the strategies are not based on the right assumptions.

Reluctant customers

Internal users don't have a choice. They can't select a different provider. They can't go out for bids and pick someone else. They can't even decide to stop using your service, since it's often mandatory! They are reluctant customers. These customers have to do business with you, but they would often rather do business with someone else.

The importance of satisfaction

After ten years of working for Gartner, I jumped the fence and became CIO for a recycling company. My main mandate was to deploy an Enterprise Resource Planning system.

I spent four years building the support organization and a project team, and delivered aggressively. We deployed the ERP in less than a year across 22 sites in two countries, and changed the operations of a business that had operated in the same way for almost a century. It was a colossal endeavour that impacted the lives of hundreds of people.

The project was a great success. Case studies have been written, we won prizes, we were asked to speak at conferences in order to provide insight into how we did such a transformation so rapidly. I was rewarded with promotions and now had responsibility for logistics (which I knew nothing about) and was leading business planning. It was a great professional success for me.

But there was still a sense of dissatisfaction in the air. Several users had that empty look of someone who'd been to hell and back. Users were reluctant to consider new projects. Old habits started creeping back into their actions, and users were by-passing the system whenever possible. Every problem was blamed on the system, even when it was obvious that it wasn't the case.

Something was missing. The project was a great success, but internally it felt like a failure. The project team felt they weren't appreciated, and that all the problems were being blamed on them. There was a crowd of angry employees, all of whom couldn't wait to see me fail.

There had to be a better way.

That's what motivated me to pursue my Masters and PhD in marketing. What if we took all the good theories and strategies that are applied in the market place but adapt them to the context of an Internal Service Provider? How can Internal Service Providers become strategic partners to the business?

This book is the result of years of research on what makes Internal Service Providers successful.

A sneak preview of some examples we'll explore:

Why married people are surprised when their spouses want a divorce
More than 55% of spouses are surprised by the decision of their partner to divorce. Does that number seem high? Hasn't there been dissatisfaction and arguments in the marriage for a while? In fact, most divorces don't end with a bang but slowly, with couples barely communicating anymore.

Think your users are satisfied because they're not complaining? Less than 5% of users complain to ISP, fearing retribution and inaction.

Why does measuring satisfaction improve satisfaction?
You probably never think about your water company. Or your phone company. The only time you think about them is when something goes wrong. The same thing happens with your users. When you ask them to think about their satisfaction outside of a crisis, it forces them to do a fair evaluation of your performance. And that makes them realize your service is actually pretty good. This phenomenon is called the mere-measurement effect.

ISPs that begin to measure satisfaction see an increase in satisfaction, even if nothing is done to improve service. But asking the users to evaluate the ISP based on specific criteria helps the users realize the quality of the service they are receiving.

What distinguishes successful dieters?
Successful dieters all have one thing in common: they weigh themselves regularly. Have you ever gone a few weeks without stepping on a scale? Perhaps you were anxious, thinking that those late night snacks ended up around your waist? Dieters that weigh themselves regularly are reminded of the severe consequences of eating that bag of chips. The next day when they weigh themselves, the needle will go higher than before, and that's not a good feeling. The daily agony of stepping on the scales actually drives their decisions for the remainder of the day.

Internal service providers that regularly measure user satisfaction are constantly reminded of their performance. ISPs that measure once a month see greater alignment within their team, since no one wants to be the reason that the needle is going in the wrong direction.

And finally perhaps the most important question of all:

How can internal service providers demonstrate business

value?

To answer this question, we will look at the concept of alignment, and the role of user satisfaction in business value. We'll also look at how ISPs can demonstrate business value without appearing to be self-promoting.

But before we get started, I'd like you to think of an Internal Service Provider that provides services to you. Perhaps it's your HR department, IT or legal. Or your cable and electricity provider, which treat you as a captive customer.

Think of the how the ISP is interacting with you and your opinion of them. How do you think your users feel about you? Let's find out.

Part 1. The Internal Service Provider

The changing role of ISP

Sex: The ultimate internal service provider

Is there anything more boring than the sex life of a married couple? I've rarely seen a movie or a TV show that promoted the merits of married sex. Typically married couples sex life is depicted as boring and dull. There are no "50 Shades of Grey" that involve a couple that's been married for 10 years. And if there were, I'm not sure it would become a best-seller.

But is married sex really that bad?

Married sex is a lot like dealing with an internal service provider. Sex in a marriage or committed relationship is a monopoly. Yes, you can always go outside to meet your needs, but that can come at a steep price. Like an internal service provider, you are subject to the capacity, skills and motivation of your provider, which can result in varying service quality and frequency. The lack of alternatives can cause some people to be frustrated and resentful if they feel the service provided doesn't match their expectations.

On the other hand, being single is like being in a free market for sex: there are a lot of single people available, and many are willing to offer their services (and I'm not even talking about professionals). There are numerous exchange platforms available to facilitate transactions (i.e. bars) and it is fairly acceptable for it to be a one-time only transaction. You can get the thrill of a new partner, access to better or different resources and the ability to change suppliers when the services offered no longer meet your requirements. And no one would bat an eye if you kept a shortlist of suppliers. Sounds like a better option than marriage, at least for sex, right?

Who has more sex: single or married?

According to many free market theories, single sex should rate higher. Much higher. The supplier is much more motivated to deliver good service, fearing the loss of the preferred supplier status. The intense competition forces everyone to raise their game and invest in new skills, processes and tools to make their service more desirable and satisfying. Single sex should clearly come out a winner, based on the free market.

But interestingly, that's not what research tells us. According to a study conducted by the Centre for Sexual Health Promotion at Indiana University, 61 percent of single people hadn't had sex within the past year, compared with 18 percent of married people. Looking specifically at people between the ages of 25 and 59, 25 percent of married people reported that they had sex two to three times per week, versus less than five percent of single people.

So despite our free-market theories, it looks like married people are having more sex than single people.

But what about service quality?

So internal service providers provide their service more often, which is easy to believe. After all, the overhead involved to initiate service for a married couple ("there's nothing good on TV, want to have sex?") is much lower than for single people (shower, get dressed, head to bar, buy drinks, try pickup lines, etc.).

But what about quality? Do these internal service providers satisfy their customers more than external providers?

It turns out internal service providers win again. People in committed relationships tend to have more satisfying sex than single people. The fact that they've been doing "business" together for a while helps them to better understand the expectations of their clients. They know the service characteristics they prefer and they know the "lay of the land," so to speak. This intimate level of understanding allows the internal service provider to adapt its service delivery in ways a new supplier wouldn't be able to. This results in clients being much more satisfied.

Looks like being an internal service provider isn't that bad after all

Although internal service providers sometimes have a bad reputation, there are also many benefits to users. Their proximity help improve frequency (something we'll call service orientation later in the book), while their understanding of their clients' needs, objectives and desires helps make the sex more satisfying (what we call business orientation). This combination differentiates internal service providers from all of the external providers out there.

Now, sex and internal service providers should probably not be compared so flippantly. For example, most couples don't give each other user a satisfaction survey every time they have sex. They also don't provide service level catalogs of what they will and will not do (although I've heard that some marriage contracts can be pretty specific). And I can't advise that you sit down with your partner with a scorecard that list the times they failed to meet performance standards. This kind of information gathering and sharing could have a dramatic impact on future frequency.

So if being married is so great for sex, why is single sex so glamorized? Because just like internal service providers, married sex suffers from a bad reputation and the misconceptions that come from being a monopoly. But you can change and improve that reputation. We'll see how in this book.

What are internal service providers?

Internal service providers are departments or groups whose role is to serve other departments. They are also known by other names: shared services, support departments, cost centres. Typical internal service providers are human resources, finance, information technology, logistics and legal. Of course many other departments qualify, depending on the company.

While internal service providers all have different areas of expertise, they do have two things in common.

1. Their clients are not the "ultimate" clients of the organization

"The client is King" is something CEOs often say when they talk about their company. They like to say that the customers are priority number one. In the case of internal service providers, their clients are not the company's clients. Internal service providers help those that help the clients; the employees and departments of the company.

This can segregate the internal service provider from the rest of the company. Users sometimes feel the ISP is not in the same boat as everyone else, since their reality is different. Their clients typically don't have to pay for their services. And internal service providers often aren't concerned about the messages and strategies from the CEO.

2. They deliver a common service to the rest of the organization

Internal service providers were created to provide economies of scale. If each business unit equipped itself with HR, IT and financial departments the costs would quickly become prohibitive. But by pooling these resources, the internal service providers can become more productive and lower costs for the organization.

Therefore a big focus of internal service providers has been to reduce their operational costs. One way they've achieved this is by delivering a common, generic service to all of their clients. As Henry Ford famously said, "You can have any colour as long as it is black."

Users, not customers

The major difference that separates internal service providers from typical external suppliers is that they have users, not customers. What's the difference? Users don't pay. Whereas companies would like their customers to buy as much as possible, most internal service organizations would actually prefer you make modest use of their services, because most internal service providers have a fixed budget. ISPs don't get any added benefit from adding new "clients," instead they end up having to stretch an already tight budget.

Encouraging users to consume more of their services would be suicide for these departments. Internal service providers want you to make reasonable use of their services, but no more. This leads internal service providers to severely restrict the services they offer and create administrative roadblocks to ensure that the resources are well distributed. Need a new computer? Fill out this long form to dissuade you from asking for too many new things in the future.

Internal service providers also don't have any competition. The great equalizer in the market place is the ability to switch suppliers. When a customer is not happy with a supplier, they can always go elsewhere. Users don't have this option. Users don't select their suppliers and they can't switch when they are not happy. Most users can't decide to buy their own work computer and have the company pay for it, just like they can't use a different insurance company for their benefits administration. IT and HR have already made these decisions for them.

Finally, users don't have a choice of whether to use the service or not. If customers aren't happy with service, they can always decide to skip the service altogether. Users don't have this luxury. Users are not happy with the timesheet system? Too bad, you have to use it if you want to get paid. Users not happy with the hotel they have to stay in when travelling for work? Too bad, the company will not reimburse you for any other hotel. Opting out is not an option for these users.

The difference between a user and a customer has not been lost on internal service providers. Many have used this power greedily, optimizing their own cost at the expense of users. ISPs have been pushing work and procedures on their users, so that some ISPs are now seen more as obstacles rather than partners. No wonder ISPs have a bad reputation.

The bad reputation of internal service providers
How many times have you heard people talking about their HR department as being cold and concerned only with productivity? Or that the IT team's software is slow and buggy and their technicians condescending and not helpful? Or legal, who are often seen as ultra-cautious bureaucrats that take the fun out of everything ("What do you mean we can't use the photocopier during the Christmas party?").

But reality is that this reputation is partly well deserved. For years, internal service providers have acted as monopolies, treating their internal users as a captive clientele. Who cares if users have nowhere else to go?

ISPs have also been under constant pressure to reduce their costs. One way they have done so is to transfer work to the users they are supposed to serve. For example, finance has pushed managing invoices and order taking to the employees, requiring them to input order information and supplier details themselves. This has allowed finance to dramatically reduce their amount of work. It also dramatically increased the users' workload, as they had to figure out accounting codes, supplier classifications, bid processes, etc. This extra work for users quickly becomes a nightmare when you only do it a few times a year.

Many internal service suppliers have also become arrogant in service delivery. Some departments earned a reputation for being unhelpful and even mean to their users. How many times have you heard the story about the computer technician asking the user if the computer is plugged in, and then making fun of users for not knowing how to solve a simple problem? Their specialization has allowed them to become more proficient in their particular area of responsibility, and they've wielded that power by making others feel incompetent.

Finally, internal service providers have strong opinions on how the business should be run. While they have these strong opinions, they don't necessarily possess the knowledge to understand how it should be run. ISPs routinely criticize the operation of other departments, telling them how they should do things. Of course, these same suppliers rarely have their own operation under control.

Expectations are changing

Taking users for granted is an attitude that no longer works. Expectations from the business are changing.

Companies used to be happy to reduce costs by centralizing shared services, they now expect a lot from their internal service suppliers:

- They expect their internal service suppliers to act like professional service organizations, delivering outstanding customer service to their users.
- ISPs need to be able to demonstrate and quantify their contribution to the business, in order to justify their budget.
- Finally, companies want their internal service providers to behave like they are part of the business, not like an external provider.

In the coming chapters we will look at these three trends and their impacts.

Trend 1. ISPs are no longer a monopoly

Why bother?

One question I often get asked is "why bother?" Internal service providers are a monopoly. Users don't have a choice. Does it make a difference if users are satisfied or not? At the end of the day, they have to use the services at their disposal. And you know what, users will never be happy. So why bother trying?

Commercial businesses have three reasons to keep customers satisfied, none of which applies to you ISPs:

1. So customers don't leave. Users don't have a choice but to get their services from you. They can't go outside or hire a different company to get services. You are a monopoly. And better yet, they are obligated to use your services. They can't even opt out. They cannot decide one day to just stop using the company's email system. It's not an option.

2. So customers buy more. You probably don't want them to use your services more. In fact, it would be great if they used them less. Less printing, less storage, less hiring. It would reduce operational costs and allow a better control of the budget.

3. So customers bring in new customers. Chances are you don't want new users, or to offer services to people outside of your organization. Your market is limited to the users you already have.

Monopolies are in the same situation as you. I don't have a choice in which electric company to use. I cannot buy my electricity from a different company, since I live in a regulated market. I can't even negotiate the price, since it is fixed by the government. All I can do is consume or not consume electricity. Of course I could use natural gas, but it is also regulated. I live in an area that has basically removed any options. Why should they care if I'm satisfied or not?

As we'll see, there are plenty of reasons ISPs should care.

Users have options

Internal service providers used to be the only game in town. Users didn't have the knowledge, skills and budget to either perform the services themselves, or go outside to acquire them. Most services had huge up-front costs (software, material, training, capital costs, etc.) that a small department could not afford. ISPs relied on cost and complexity to keep their advantage over their internal clients.

But this advantage is slowly eroding. Options are now becoming available for users to replace services offered by internal service providers. Users are much more knowledgeable and are no longer "hostage" to their ISP. In fact, users are often better equipped at home than at work. Business units are a lot more knowledgeable about the tools and approaches that used to be the territory of the internal service providers. In fact, some business units now hire employees with backgrounds in their internal service provider's area of expertise (IT, HR, finance, logistics, legal, etc.)

Outside suppliers have leveraged the frustration users have toward their internal service provider to develop new solutions. A new breed of suppliers is advertising directly to users. What's the benefit? You can use our services without having to involve your ISP. And this message works. Salesforce.com, a leading provider of CRM solutions in the Cloud, now has 100,000 customers based on this value proposition.

Example: Hiring without HR

HR used to be the only way a department could hire employees. HR held the keys of the recruiting kingdom: the payroll. You couldn't hire anyone unless HR had approved it, and in most cases HR took care of the entire hiring process.

But new options are now available. Two platforms are increasingly popular for hiring short-term staff: elance.com and odesk.com. These platforms link suppliers and buyers from all over the world in a HR trading platform. You need a specialist to develop a web site? Contractors from Pakistan will be glad to help you out. You need to design a new brochure? A nice group from Eastern Europe is more than willing to assist you. One of the key advantages of these platforms is that you never have to hire anyone; it is all done through a vendor-supplier relationship, payable by credit card.

These types of platforms change the game for recruiting. It is now easy for recruiters to post jobs, filter through possible resumes and even try out different candidates. No payroll hassles, no issues managing performance and coaching. If you aren't satisfied with the work, you simply end the contract. While it is not appropriate for all situations, it has changed the balance of power tremendously between the users and the HR department.

Example: Bring your own device

Another example of the power shift is Bring Your Own Device (BYOD). This trend started appearing in IT departments when users wanted to start using iPhones and iPads at work. Most IT departments were reluctant to authorize these devices, fearing that it would trigger a massive expense. After all, when a new phone is introduced, for some reason the number of old phones breaking, being dropped in toilets and "lost" increases dramatically.

IT departments resisted at first, claiming issues with security or corporate standards. But users would not accept ITs resistance and started bringing in their own devices. IT departments lost control; it was a losing battle. So how did they manage the situation?

IT has more fully developed the concept of "bring your own device." Buy whatever you want, and they'll give you access to the network. But you are on your own; they won't provide support for your device (or very minimal support). Some IT departments even saw this as an opportunity to reduce costs. Instead of providing a device to everyone, they would give employees an allocation of funds and let them purchase what they wanted.

You are being compared to others

Users are becoming more and more sophisticated in what they expect from their suppliers. They purchase technology for their home (cable, internet, computers, iPads), they purchase services (lawn care, cleaning services, repairs) and they get support from providers.

In addition, employees are more and more mobile, changing jobs frequently and seeing how other internal service providers deliver their services. You've probably heard quite a few times, "In my previous company, we used to have…"

Users are always comparing services. They compare them to the commercial providers they use, compare them to their past employers, and compare them to their expectations (right or wrong) of how you should be serving them. They no longer feel privileged to have access to your services; it is now normal. And as such, they are expecting you to step up, and deliver your services in the same manner others do.

User acceptance is an important part of project success

User adoption and acceptance is a significant factor of success when deploying new initiatives. In addition, user involvement has been identified as a critical success factor for many years. Change management has evolved to specifically handle the adoption and acceptance aspects of project management, and consulting firms offer specialized services in user involvement and adoption.

User satisfaction will dictate how users adapt and their attitudes toward their ISP will guide how easily they adapt. So how do we determine a user's attitude? The easiest way is through user satisfaction. Satisfied users will tend to approach new initiatives with a more positive outlook, since they already successfully use the ISPs services and see value from them. They understand that new initiatives will require some changes in the way they work, and they are more willing to invest the time and effort required to advance through the learning curve.

On the other hand, unsatisfied users will actively avoid using a new system or process. They will wait until forced to do so, and even then will resist every step of the way.

ISPs can no longer use the "build it and they will come" approach. It no longer works. Users must be actively engaged in the project from beginning to end.

Trend 2. ISPs have to demonstrate business value

The new breed of services require employee participation

ISP services have traditionally been focused on process optimization. Users were merely a cog in the system, inputting information so that the process could function properly. For example, in an order-taking process the sales person would input the order, which would then feed production planning, which in turn feeds purchasing, etc. The data entered by each participant serves to feed the next step. In processes the data is mandatory, when the data is missing the process stops. Getting users to comply was easy; if they didn't the work doesn't get done.

As services have evolved, we've begun using them differently. Nowhere is this change more apparent than in CRM systems. A customer relationship management (CRM) system has value only if and when front-line employees input all of their interactions with customers. For example, my bank should know that I called last week for information regarding a new mortgage, that I went to the ATM five times in the last two weeks, and that they sent me two promotional letters in the last month. The value comes from the information itself, information entered by the users.

But to be effective, a CRM system needs to be fed with relevant data. CRMs don't break down when data isn't entered. If the customer service representative doesn't log my call, they will still be able to serve me the next time I call. The only impact will be a system that is less reliable and less informative, but nothing will actually break. This lack of consequences makes it very difficult to "police" the use of the system.

But we can always force them!

What happens when we force users to use a new CRM system? Hsieh, J.J.P. and Petter decided to find out. They analyzed the deployment of a CRM in a Chinese bank, in order to assess the impact of mandating its use. Specifically, they wanted to know if user satisfaction with a new system has an impact on the quality of the service delivered to the bank's customers.

To gain answers, they evaluated different factors. The first factor was embodied service knowledge, or how knowledgeable an agent is with the job functions. We know that more knowledgeable individuals tend to deliver better service, since they can typically answer questions accurately and quickly, and guide customers toward a resolution.

The second factor assessed was job dedication, or how motivated the agents are in doing their job. This measure was assessed by supervisors using a standardized questionnaire.

These factors were studied before, during and after the deployment of the CRM system.

Forcing works, but only if they want to

The study provided some interesting results. It is clear that forcing users to use a new CRM is a viable method, since most users complied with the new processes. This is not surprising, given that management was very committed to implementing the system and employees would have faced disciplinary action if they refused to use it (we're talking about China here).

The researchers also found that employees who were satisfied with the new system tended to see improvements in the quality of service they provided. The CRM provided more tools and information which allowed them to do their job more effectively, the reason for using a CRM in the first place.

However, employees dissatisfied with the new system tended to provide worse service, even if the employee had been a good performer prior.

Cognitive dissonance

One factor that came into play was cognitive dissonance. Cognitive dissonance is when people's behaviour does not match their beliefs. The brain doesn't like having conflicting beliefs, and will try to rectify the situation by seeking a new balance.

In the case of the dissatisfied employees, users are forced to use a system they believe is inadequate and that will provide a lower level of service. Therefore, to remove the cognitive dissonance, they lower their service level without even realizing it. This brings their beliefs and behaviour back into equilibrium.

Cognitive dissonance can harm the trust that employees have of management. The dissatisfied employees wonder why management would deploy this system if they knew it would lower service? Does management not believe customer service is important?

Satisfaction matters

This study showed that in implementing new processes, employee or user satisfaction is as important as job dedication and service knowledge. Poor user satisfaction had a direct impact on customer service, and thus customer satisfaction.

Internal service providers can no longer hide behind the idea that they are a back-office function. ISP's initiatives and processes have a direct impact on customers. As businesses begin to realize the customer impact, they ask their ISPs to step up and deliver value.

The need to demonstrate value

Internal service providers used to be perfectly happy helping to improve the company's productivity. They would implement projects to reduce headcount or remove routine, unnecessary work by automating, simplifying or consolidating tasks.

But shrinking margins bring shrinking budgets. Every business unit and department is pressured to do more with less, and budgets are cut or frozen. If the value a department provides isn't clear, then it becomes difficult to resist budget cuts. ISPs find themselves in a situation where they don't have sufficient resources to start new initiatives, and can barely sustain their existing services.

Holding the keys is no longer enough

Some ISPs tried to leverage their position of authority over their domain. The ISP could control what was happening, define standards, and they knew what could and couldn't be done.

This kind of ISP power is slowly eroding as business units prefer to seek forgiveness rather than ask permission. Internal service providers that don't generate value can see themselves excluded from important decisions, discussions and orientations. Isn't it common for ISPs to complain that they hear about initiatives only when everything is already decided? Most likely the business units making the decisions don't see the value in involving the ISPs sooner. In fact, they may even avoid them altogether if the ISP has a reputation for slowing things down.

If you don't do it, someone else will

There is an army of suppliers knocking at your CEO's door to replace you and your team. External suppliers have developed countless offerings to outsource operations. Cheaper, faster, better tools. Competing with external suppliers on cost alone is nearly impossible, primarily because they typically have much bigger economies of scale than any ISP. Even if they are not cheaper, their promise of surprise-free costs (they are under a fixed-price contract) is often very enticing.

Do you think you are safe because your company doesn't believe in outsourcing? There is also a trend to lump internal service providers together into shared services groups, to further reduce overhead costs. By combining all "commodity" services together, the economies of scale go up by reducing staff and leaders.

Any internal service provider that cannot clearly demonstrate its value will be treated as a commodity. But how do you demonstrate value?

The challenges of measuring value

Sorry, business executives don't think about you.

We'd all like to think that we are an essential part of the company and that things would grind to a halt if we weren't there. You might very well be essential. You probably provide services that would cripple the organization if they were to stop. But the reality is that business executives, your internal clients and your users don't spend any time thinking about you. They are busy with daily operational execution and don't have the time to worry about the value of the services you provide.

Unless you screw up. Then everyone will be thinking about you. They will talk about all the times you made mistakes or that your service was not available. They will review your budget and wonder how come the service is so poor given the amount of money that is being wasted in your department. Everyone will suddenly become very interested in the status of your projects, whether you are meeting budget numbers, and the state of your services.

They don't understand what you do

Does your mom really understand what you do for a living? Probably not. She knows you are important, she's probably very proud of you, but she has no idea what it is exactly that you do.

This is also true for your clients. Their lack of interest doesn't mean they don't care. The major problem is that most executives don't know what it is you do every day. They understand the broad lines, that you manage HR , technology or take care of the legal "stuff." But they don't understand what skills or what resources it takes on a day-to-day basis to perform your functions.

This lack of understanding prevents them from effectively judging the quality of your work. To circumvent this, some ISPs have decided to measure their contribution objectively.

Value is in the eye of the beholder

Business value is difficult to measure. Some internal service organizations have tried a variety of techniques to measure and demonstrate their business value.

One of the most popular approaches is to benchmark operational costs. Several companies specialize in benchmarking internal service provider budgets and can provide comparative metrics on all aspects of ISP operational performance. This allows ISPs to evaluate their productivity compared to their peers in general and to their industry specifically. Unfortunately, benchmarking doesn't really work for demonstrating value; it only confirms that the ISP isn't wasting money. Benchmarking doesn't show that the work the ISP is doing actually contributes to the needs of the organization.

Another popular approach is the use of return on investment metrics. ROI metrics can show that your activities and initiatives deliver more than they cost, which is a fairly straightforward way to demonstrate value. But it turns out that ROI doesn't work all that well either. Measuring the benefits of ISP projects can sometimes become very complicated, even causing turf wars between ISPs and business units as to who's created the benefit.

Elaborate tools and frameworks have also been devised to measure the impact of an ISP using a variety of business metrics. But these approaches have also been difficult to implement, since the cost of maintaining the metrics and framework can be more costly than the benefit provided. And frankly, few business executives understand or believe them.

Unfortunately, value is in the eye of the beholder. There are no financial measures or approaches that will satisfy the concerns of all business managers. But there is a measure that comes close: user satisfaction.

User Satisfaction as a barometer of the business value

ISPs are seen as a cost centre in most companies. One of the major challenges that ISP leaders face is justifying their budget. I keep hearing things like, "ISPs are like a black hole, we keep pouring money in it!" or, "No matter how much we give them, they still ask for more!"

But what is business value really?

First, internal service providers must define what kind of value they bring to the business. For some, being a low cost provider is how they contribute, while others contribute by providing new, innovative solutions.

But since value depends on the client's satisfaction, we have a simpler definition:

"Does the ISP perform the role that is expected of it?"

Although it may appear simplistic, this definition accurately represents   the concerns of the business executive. An organization that works hard to optimize their costs and regularly benchmark themselves to their peers might still fail to meet expectations if the business is expecting someone to help them innovate and try new solutions. On the other hand, an organization going through a massive business transformation project can be disappointed in an ISP that delivers high-touch service but lacks the leadership to push new systems and processes.

In Part 2, we'll see how different personality profiles contribute to the goals of the organization.

Satisfaction as a surrogate measure of value

Benchmarks, ROI and frameworks do a poor job of measuring expectations. They primarily rate ISPs against an artificial standard of performance that may or may not be the expectations of the clients. This is why these measures often fail.

But one measure captures expectations very well: satisfaction. After all, the definition of satisfaction is the difference between the service delivered and service expected. You deliver more than users are expecting? Satisfaction goes up. You deliver less, satisfaction goes down.

The research literature has clearly shown through numerous studies that user satisfaction is the best predictor of value. Satisfaction captures all of the client's expectations, service delivery performance and client understanding all in one easy to measure metrics.

Trend 3. ISPs are part of the business

The difference between a 15$ and a 200$ haircut

Why are some people willing to spend up to 200$ for a haircut while others will only pay 15$?

The service experience for a 15$ haircut is pretty straightforward. You show up and wait for a few minutes since they don't take appointments. Once a hairdresser is free you sit down, explain that you want to refresh your haircut a little bit and the hairdresser gets to work, asking a few questions to clarify what you want. While the overall interaction could be very social and interesting, the level of involvement of the hairdresser in the solution is usually fairly limited: you're the one that specified exactly what you want in very technical terms (shorter sides, side part, etc.).

Oftentimes, the hairdresser has no idea what the client's objectives really are. Does he want to look younger? Is he getting ready for a big date? The 15$ haircut is transactional and can be considered a commodity; any hairdresser with the right skills can take the client's requirements and deliver a successful haircut. That's because the specifications are very clear. But what happens when clients don't know what they want?

The 200$ haircut is a world apart from the 15$ experience. The location tends to be nicer, they might offer wine or champagne to their clients and the ambiance is relaxing, similar to a spa. But the real difference is the hairdresser's involvement. When someone goes to a 200$ hairdresser, the specifications tend to be fuzzy, to the point of being almost non-existent. The client will typically say something like "I want to look younger" or "I need a new look." It is then the responsibility of the hairdresser to question the client to determine the style, the length, how cutting-edge, how much time they have to prepare in the morning, etc.

The hairdresser is responsible for designing a solution to meet the client's objectives. Based on some vague terms and likes/dislikes, the hairdresser finds a solution (a haircut) that will meet the client's demands. This requires a high level of efficient communication, after all, once the hair is cut it is pretty hard to fix. But it also requires a high-level of understanding of current trends and fashion styles, an understanding of physiology and morphology to understand which haircut will be becoming. And it's for this level of involvement that these upscale hairdressers can demand an order of magnitude more for their services. And clients are happy to pay it.

Understanding the business

Most internal service providers act like 15$ hairdressers. They have taken the requests and needs from the business and delivered them as quickly and efficiently as possible. Shorter hair? Done. Need a new hire? Done. They focus on fulfilling as many requests as possible to meet as many of their users' needs as they can. But this transactional relationship doesn't work anymore for their clients.

A study conducted by the Harvard Business Review showed that over half of CEOs were dissatisfied with the role of their internal service providers, feeling that they didn't "get it." They felt their ISPs weren't acting as partners, as if they didn't understood the business they were supposed to help. They were giving 15$ haircut while the business wanted a new look.

The situation is so severe, that half the CEOs anticipated major changes in the leadership of their internal service providers. In the last five years, we've seen a major trend where leaders of internal service providers come from a company's business units rather than from the department. It was hoped that this change would improve the ISP's understanding of the business' needs.

Simply being good at cutting hair doesn't work anymore.

Living in the business

Internal service providers have been operating as if they are not actually part of the business. An internal service provider leader is first and foremost a business leader. Its job is to help the company meet its objectives. The means to do so varies, for example it will do so through either technology, RH, finance, legal, etc. But the means are only secondary.

Several years ago, Singer, the manufacturer of sewing machines, wanted to start selling on the web. Their IT department took the initiative to setup a web store (which was pretty complicated at the time) and wanted to make it available to the public. But the marketing vice-president stopped them just in time. Singer had divided its authorized merchants into territories, and selling on the internet would have breached their contracts. It took six more months to negotiate dividend payments with the stores before they could sell on the internet, and required revamping the web store completely. The IT department could have caused a major conflict between Singer and its authorized dealers because they didn't understand the company's sales channel.

A business leader needs to understand key financial results (to the extent that executives share them) and should know basic metrics about the company (revenues, profits, profit margin, number of sites, number of employees) as well as being able to answer the following questions:

1. How does the company make money?
2. Who are the clients and what are their needs?
3. How do you reach your clients?
4. What products/services are offered to fulfill the need?
5. What's unique about the products and services?
6. Who is the competition and how do the products compare?
7. What kind of team does the company need to be a success?
8. What operation/infrastructure is required for growth?
9. What is the growth plan and how far along are they on the plan?
10. What is the plan for the next year?

The number of ISP leaders that cannot answer these simple questions is surprisingly high. Most leaders in other business units could probably answer those in their sleep, whether they are responsible for the results or not. ISP leaders can't afford to live outside the organization anymore; they need to step up to the same standards as everyone else.

Managing the details

Just like the hairdresser, companies are looking for partners that can take a general vision and handle the details. They no longer want to have to dictate all of their requirements in prioritized lists. They are looking for their partner to do the grunt work of understanding the business, understanding their own field and bridging the two.

Your company wants to grow? Then you should already know what the impact will be on your infrastructure, on your services, staffing and costs. But you should also understand what it will mean for your internal clients, and develop solutions to address these issues ahead of time. Will they require communication solutions? Massive hiring? New languages? Provide large scale training? You can help your clients identify all of these new requirements, and then take the steps to proactively solve them.

Clients want a new look. It's up to the ISP to find which one.

Understanding the industry

There is an old joke between ISP leaders. A business executive reads about a cool trend in an in-flight magazine or the chief in operations overhears casual conversation about technology while on the slopes, and the ISP leader's email box starts to fill up. Or even worse is when they go to conferences, vendors pitching tons of new solutions and approaches. So when a business leader starts travelling, ISP brace for the deluge.

Companies today operate in a very dynamic marketplace, and whether they are in competitive markets or in non-profit (such as public sector for example), the need to keep up with the industry is everywhere. Organizations, and their leaders, are constantly challenged to outperform one another and they are continually benchmarked to compare their productivity, management and innovation. One way company leaders can to do this is to better leverage the service and solutions that internal service providers can deliver.

Understand what others are doing

Most business executives are pretty savvy about what their competitors or peers in their industry are doing in term of business practices. They read industry magazines, talk to one another and even hire consultants to stay up-to-date. But chances are they do not track the specifics of your domain. They are typically not fully aware of all the software application others are implementing, new trends in recruitment or approaches to contract negotiation.

This is where internal service providers have fallen short. While most ISP leaders understand new trends in their area of expertise, they do not put that understanding in the context of their own industry. What's the percentage of companies in your industry that have a CRM or a talent management application? The majority? Half?

None?

Businesses now expect internal service providers to stay up-to-date on these trends. Not necessarily to jump on the bandwagon of their competitors, but to understand where others are going and what differentiates them from your own organization.

Successful partnerships

Businesses are also expecting a different approach than a simple client-supplier relationship. They want their ISPs to be there, side-by-side with them to tackle their toughest business challenges. They expect their ISP partners to be focused on the same objectives and to share the same drive to achieve them.

But ISPs have historically been difficult to partner with. Their constant focus on productivity and managing the continuous flow of requests has made them more like a catalog-shopping company than a real partner. Send your request by mail and we'll ship it to you in 4 to 6 weeks.

Let's look at three characteristics that successful ISPs are developing in order to become partners.

Partners are easy to engage

Departments often resent ISPs that require forms to be completed every time they interact with them. Want to look at a new potential project? Please fill-out the project submission form first. Want to consider hiring a new employee? Please fill-out a personnel requisition form. Everyone understands the need to put processes in place to help manage and track work, but at some point these processes begin to be a way for ISPs to distance themselves from their clients.

Successful internal service providers are developing mechanisms to make it easier for them to be involved in the day-to-day activities of their clients. They schedule regular meetings, participate in their client's departmental meetings and share information regularly to keep the communication channels open. And while they need to maintain a minimum of processes to manage their workload, they strive to make these as painless as possible for their clients.

Partners know their clients

No single ISP leader can be expected to know everything about its clients and have the time to develop meaningful relationships with everyone. The complexity of their service delivery combined with the difference between business units would make the task impossible. But, the ISP needs to understand the key objectives and challenges for each client, and more importantly, understand the entire scope of service it delivers to them.

Some internal service providers have implemented the concept of business relationship managers (BRM) to act as a liaison between the clients and the various parts of their service organization. Similar to the concept of commercial relationship managers, BRMs act as a single point of contact for everything related to the ISP. Clients don't need to deal with various managers and professionals who may quickly pass the ball around when it doesn't fall in their respective area of responsibility.

Regardless if it is a full-time position or simply a responsibility added to someone's position, having this role helps tremendously in understanding clients. But of course, understanding clients only helps if we're proactive about adapting solutions to meet their needs.

Partners want their client to succeed

A real partner won't succeed if you fail. Business units resent when internal service providers get recognition and rewards when the rest of the business is not meeting its objectives.

It is now common for internal service providers to have the same business objectives as the rest of the organization. The bonuses their leader may receive is often dependent on the same business metrics of the company's other leaders. Although some debate the effectiveness of this technique, it does help provide a common alignment to the priorities of the organization.

But whether this alignment is enforced or not, internal service providers want their clients to succeed. They need to work diligently to allow their clients to meet their objectives and deliver on their commitments.

Building partnerships

ISPs want to become a business partner. They have their own ideas on how to reduce costs and increase sales. ISPs want to be at the executive table and voice their opinion on what is happening in the organization.

Some companies welcome ISPs to the table with wide open arms. Some organizations go as far as having ISPs play an important leadership role at the executive table. Yet other organization's execs won't even answer their ISP's calls. Why is that? Because those ISPs don't have any credibility.

Credibility is difficult to gain and easy to lose. Let's take the phone company as an example. As a consultant I do a significant part of my business on the phone. I call clients, I have conference calls, I make sales calls. The phone is a very important tool for my business, without it my life would be extremely complicated. But do I consider my phone as a strategic part of my business? I'm not sure.

If, for instance, the phone company called me and said, "Simon, we want to help you grow your business, and we think we can help you become a better consultant." Chances are my first reaction would be "Why don't you start by making sure my phone works every time I pick it up?"

See, I've had serious coverage issues with my phone. I'm sure I'm not the only one with these issues, but the phone is such an important element of my work. When it doesn't work flawlessly, it's annoying and could affect my business. If they can't deliver something as simple as reliable service, what makes them think they have the credibility to become my partner?

Perhaps it's over the top to ask for perfection, but when it comes to business service, that's what I want. But I'll settle for very, very good. If the phone company doesn't deliver very, very good service, I simply won't trust them. So the day they call me to become a partner, I'll remind them how they have failed me in the past few months and ask them politely to fix their service, before they think about doing anything else.

Satisfaction is a measure of how well you meet their needs
User satisfaction provides a great measure of how well you are meeting their needs at the various levels. By setting and managing expectations you provide a framework in which users can shape their needs. If you explicitly say that you will not support mobile devices because as an organization we feel it is too expensive, then the users will shape their expectations accordingly. It is not a failure to execute but simply a corporate direction (one they might not agree with but can probably understand). But if IT says it is supporting mobile devices but do so poorly, then users will see it as a failure to execute.

Satisfaction is the measure of your rights earned.
Therefore, user satisfaction is a good representation of the levels you've achieved. An ISP with satisfied users will have greater opportunities to contribute to the business, since they will be seen as good providers. On the other hand, dissatisfied users will clearly point out what needs to be fixed before the ISP can play a greater role in the business, providing a clear path for the future.

Satisfaction matters

The common theme that comes out of these trends is the need to focus on user satisfaction.

Satisfaction helps ISPs deliver quality service that will be used and recognized, it helps demonstrate business value since IT executives rely on employee satisfaction as a barometer of value, and it helps earn the right to become a strategic partner. In the next pages, we will see exactly what satisfaction is and how to achieve it.

What is satisfaction?

Reducing satisfaction to reduce costs?

I once had a client with an amazing user satisfaction rating. He had well over a 97% satisfaction index. Surprisingly though, he was slightly concerned about this score. The IT organization had suffered from credibility issues in the past and spared no cost to try and remedy the situation. The results were staggering, but the executive wondered if perhaps this high user satisfaction was costing him a small fortune.

His question to me was simple: what would be the financial impact of reducing satisfaction to 90% instead of 97%? The score would still be very good; 90% is something that most organizations only dream of achieving. He believed that reducing the level of satisfaction would reduce his costs dramatically. So he wanted me to evaluate what he could cut in terms of cost, while accepting that it would have an impact on satisfaction.

Although I was surprised by his request, I understood where he was coming from. Everyone wants to cut costs, and he was willing to sacrifice a small amount of satisfaction in order to achieve his objective. So I started digging.

But a little bit of history first. When this client started five years ago, IT at the company was in a state of utter and complete disarray, had no credibility and was often the butt of cruel jokes. Every project was met with skepticism, hostility and contempt. Users were disgruntled, business leaders unsupportive and IT wasn't able to do its job properly. It was clear that the situation was unsustainable and something needed to be done. Quickly.

They decided to tackle the issue very aggressively without really understanding what drives user satisfaction at the company. Their thinking was "We'll give the users what they want, even if it costs a lot." To do so they started carrying high levels of inventory so that hardware was always available. They established an aggressive evergreening policy so no one would have a computer that was older than three years old. Help-desk support was made available 24/7, so users would always have someone to reach in case of a problem if they were working late, through the night or even at home. They changed the specifications of their equipment so computers were faster and had greater performance. Their policy became, "Whatever the user wants."

This policy had a positive impact on user satisfaction. Users had been accustomed to an environment in which IT would constantly say no and provided old, beat up equipment. Now users' were getting the latest and greatest. But the new policy was very expensive. All the benchmarks were in the upper percentile, significantly more expensive than peer companies. However, we knew that higher cost doesn't necessarily drive satisfaction. In fact (as we'll see later on) it is possible to increase satisfaction while maintaining or even reducing cost.

Obviously, the first thing I did was to identify the main cost drivers. It was clear that a lot of the mechanisms that had been put in place to meet client satisfaction were costing a bundle. I then looked at the drivers of client satisfaction in the organization. I was surprised, to say the least, that a big part of what they had put in place had little impact on user satisfaction.

Elements that had the greatest impact were the regular meetings with business leaders and users, and the service catalog. Every month,

IT would publish its performance scorecard and sit one-on-one with their business leaders to discuss the scorecard. They also provided mechanisms for users to voice their concerns and needs. Of course the basic IT needs of the organization were met, but the biggest impact was going from a culture of "We know what's best for you" to one of "let's talk about what you need and how we performed." This exercise in identifying and managing expectations allowed the IT organization to clearly understand what was required to meet expectations, and manage them over time.

At the end of the exercise, instead of coming up with a list of things to eliminate, we set up a governance team that allowed the users to make the decisions. With IT's guidance, they eliminated a number of things from IT's list of services and also relaxed performance standards significantly. As a result, IT reduced its costs and user satisfaction was barely affected.

This feel-good example demonstrates three things: user satisfaction is not necessarily expensive, it is not about giving users everything they want, and user satisfaction is first a communications exercise.

Your morning coffee and satisfaction

We all know when we are satisfied. Every day you have countless service interactions. You pick up your morning coffee at Starbucks, you drop-off your dry-cleaning, you do some grocery shopping. Each time you have such a service interaction you know very well if you are satisfied or not.

You probably never have said to yourself, "I will pick-up my morning cup of coffee and I expect it to be hot and delicious. I expect the service to be quick, the barista to be courteous and smiling and I expect to quickly be on my way."

You probably don't have a checklist of services you check off as satisfied or not, and then give your service providers a score. But yet, this is what is happening. Some mornings you probably tell yourself "Wow, service was awful today." And if you tell yourself this too often, then you switch where you get your coffee.

The person in front of you might have slightly different criteria. Perhaps they are not in a hurry and speed is not that important. Perhaps the taste of the coffee is their most important criteria, and they would make a detour to get the coffee they like. The person behind you might care only about price and they visit this place because it is cheap. Their criteria for satisfaction are different. So how can the coffee place define what satisfies their users?

The American Customer Satisfaction Index tracks the customer satisfaction of major chains in North America. In 2012, it found that Starbucks customer satisfaction dropped 5 points to 76%, while Dunkin Donuts scored 79%. Starbucks and Dunkin Donuts are clearly two different types of customer experiences. Dunkin Donuts is a no-frills, cost-conscious coffee place while Starbucks aims to provide a customer experience. Thus, we see that either Starbucks is not as good as it once was at delivering a rich coffee experience, or the users' expectations have changed.

Intuitively, satisfaction is very simple. So why is it such a complex topic?

To find out, we'll further look at what is satisfaction and investigate the two variables in this equation: the service delivered and the service expected.

Defining satisfaction
Satisfaction is defined as the attitude users have toward a service rendered. This attitude can be either positive or negative in varying degrees. But this definition doesn't help us understand how satisfaction is formed.

To understand this, we'll use a different definition, one that is more in line with how ISPs operate. Simply put, satisfaction is the difference between the service delivered and the service expected. If the service delivered is better than the service expected by users, then they will be satisfied. On the other hand, if the service delivered is inferior to their expectations, users will be dissatisfied.

Satisfaction = Service Delivered - Service Expected

Satisfaction comes in degrees. If the service expected is only marginally inferior to the service expected, the user will still be satisfied, being tolerant for small mistakes and issues. Users' expectations are never precise to begin with and they typically allow for a very large margin of error.

It sounds very simple in theory, but the complexity starts when we analyze the two elements of this equation: the service delivered and the service expected.

Service delivered
The first component of satisfaction is the actual service delivered by the internal service provider. Intuitively, we can all agree that if the service delivered is poor or inconsistent, then users will be dissatisfied. If you go to a coffee shop and the coffee is cold, they are out of sugar, and the milk is sour, then chances are you will be greatly dissatisfied with the service received. Delivering a great product is essential to satisfying customers.

Most of the work done by internal service providers focus on improving the actual service delivered. This includes providing new, innovative solutions to their users, increasing hours of service, responding to requests promptly, and responding to the users' needs. This is an important part of the service delivery; after all, if the service provided isn't working properly, nothing else will really make a difference to improve satisfaction.

How it is delivered

But equally important is how a service is delivered. Imagine a coffee shop that serves the best coffee in the world, just the right temperature with a rich aroma and the perfect amount of foam on top. Sounds pretty good, doesn't it? But now, imagine that coffee served by a rude, arrogant barista who is dismissive and obviously annoyed by your constant requests. Chances are your satisfaction would plummet, even if the coffee was perfect!

Service orientation, the way services are delivered by an internal service provider, is just as important as the services themselves. Most companies hire frontline support staff based on their technical skills, and rightly so—it takes an enormous amount of knowledge and skills to diagnose and fix issues. However, research by Jia and Reich has shown that customer service skills are twice as important for user satisfaction as technical skills (27% vs. 15%).

Customer service is twice as important as technical skills for user satisfaction

Therefore, users consider both the service received (the "what") and also how well the service was provided (the "how"). Was the support person polite, courteous, and respectful of my time? Was he arrogant, did he make me feel incompetent, did he belittle me, etc.?

Historically, internal service providers have not focused much on "how" the service was delivered. As long as the service was provided, who really cared? Users did. This kind of attitude contributed to the poor reputation of internal service providers in many organizations. ISP leaders have reacted, and many provide customer service training to their employees to ensure that the way their employees act in front of their internal clients is in line with the image the ISP wants to convey to the business.

But the service delivered is only half of the equation. Let's look at the service expected.

Service expected

Walt Disney has an amazing track record of satisfying its clients. Well, its "guests" as Disney likes to call them. Everything Disney does is with the customer in mind. It starts when you arrive, where a small army of parking attendants guide you to your parking spot (you don't get to choose, you park where they tell you). No running around trying to find an empty spot, going from one lane to another. You are simply guided very efficiently to a lane of empty spots, and everyone parks one next to another until it is full.

Then inside, employees (they call them cast members) greet you with large smiles and guide you to the attraction of our choice. While I was there with my family we were standing in the middle of the place looking at a map, when a cleaning crew member came and asked me if I needed directions. Someone who's job was to shine garbage cans (which is pretty incredible in itself) offered to show me the way without having to ask.

There is no doubt Disney's service is amazing. They work very hard to make the entire experience unforgettable. But one thing Disney does better than anyone else is to set expectations about their service. Disney never promises something they cannot deliver. In fact they go out of their way to set the right level of expectations. For example, they have huge electronic billboards that show the wait time for each ride, so you know well in advance how long it will take you to get in. The description of their restaurants always includes a menu so there are no surprises, and they always specify what kind of service to expect (sit-down vs. fast-food, for example). Want to see a mascot? An employee manages the line and explains to you very clearly how to proceed, so there is no confusion and it is fair for everyone.

This focus on managing expectations is what separates Disney from other amusement parks.

Service expected and ISPs

This is where most ISPs fail. As part of our research, we've seen several organizations that worked tirelessly to deliver great service, were very responsive, and had amazing customer service skills, yet consistently failed to satisfy users. They were delivering great services, but their users were expecting even more.

Users have certain expectations when they receive a service. Whether it's the level of responsiveness, their level of involvement in fixing the problem, or the attitude and skills of the support person. Each of these components vary from user to user and from time to time, making user expectations difficult to understand.

Successful ISPs don't leave expectations to chance. Who knows what kind of expectations the user will have, and whether they are realistic? Instead, successful ISPs proactively set expectations well in advance. And they do it the same way Disney does. Calling HR to get a new hire? They will specify to you right away that it typically takes two weeks to get all the steps done. Does that work for you? You know right away what kind of delay to expect and you reset your expectations as a user accordingly.

There are many ways to set expectations: service catalogues, messages at the time of a transaction, communications at large, etc. The point is for ISPs to put as much energy in making sure users have the right level of expectations as they do into delivering great service.

Measuring satisfaction

Now that we know what satisfaction is, let's see how we can actually measure it. But first, do we even need to measure satisfaction?

I would know if my users were dissatisfied

It seems most people would know if their partner was unhappy in their marriage. There would be signs, conflicts, screaming and perhaps a few plates thrown. I'm sure we could expect to see some high-drama, tears and perhaps even some good old violence when a couple is about to divorce. After all, it is a very emotional decision.

It turns out that isn't the case. Research shows that most marriages that fail are not high-conflict marriages, and 55% of the partners are surprised by the decision of their spouse to divorce. These couples didn't have ecstatic marriages by any means, but they didn't fight all the time either. The status of the relationship was clearly not the same for both parties, to the point where one person thought things were fine while the other was filing for divorce.

What does this have to do with ISPs? It simply shows that people are poor judges when they evaluate their relationship, especially when there are no open conflicts. "Business as usual" relationships doesn't mean that all is well; it simply means that no one is openly complaining about it.

Most users don't complain when they are dissatisfied

Research also shows that most users don't complain when they are dissatisfied. There are a lot of reasons for this:
- They believe it won't change anything
- They believe it will take too much effort for little gain
- They are afraid of retribution
- They don't know how to file a complaint

In fact, statistics shows that less than 4% of customers complain when they are dissatisfied, and this statistic is even worse in the case of B2B relationships.

No news is not good news. The only way to know if users are satisfied is to ask them.

Satisfaction surveys

ISPs use different strategies to measure and manage satisfaction:

- Gossip - The least reliable form of user feedback, yet the most destructive. Gossip about an ISPs performance (or lack thereof) can have a dramatic impact on user satisfaction.
- User complaints - User complaints are a great source of data for ISP managers as it provides an opportunity to correct a failure in service delivery. Unfortunately less than 4% of dissatisfied users typically complain, the other dissatisfied 96% prefer to say nothing. And users will not complaint if they feel it will not yield any results, so ISPs without any complaints may not be as good as they think they are. Complaints are not a great source of feedback to judge the overall satisfaction of users.
- Service orientation assessment - The service orientation assessment is a way for ISPs to evaluate the presence of pre-requisites to satisfy users. It allows ISPs to estimate what would be the satisfaction of their users without running a formal survey. Combined with a user survey, it gives both the symptoms (the survey results) and the diagnostic (the assessment).
- Annual user satisfaction surveys - Over half of ISPs perform at least an annual user satisfaction survey. Using diagnostic questions, the annual survey aims to measure the attitude of users toward the services delivered and typically tries to understand why users gave a high or low rating. Since it is done only once a year, the survey tends to be long and include questions that may not be relevant to all users. The major issue with yearly surveys is that ISP managers tend to forget about satisfaction for the remainder of the year.
- Monthly user satisfaction surveys - The monthly user satisfaction survey is similar to the annual survey except that it divides the users into 12 groups and surveys a different group each month, so no individual users get surveyed more than

once or twice a year. The survey tends to be shorter and include more dynamic questions; questions that vary from month to month in order to better understand a specific issue or the impact of a project. The monthly survey also reinforces the importance of user satisfaction to ISP managers since the surveys come out at the same frequency as the budget numbers, keeping results on the table each month. Monthly results allow ISPs to identify which initiatives really made a difference on satisfaction and which didn't.

- Post-transaction survey - A post-transaction survey (or ticket close survey) is a survey that is sent every time a transaction has been completed. For example, some ISPs send a survey to every (or a percentage of) user that has sent a request to the help-desk. The ticket close survey provides on-going feedback on the service quality and gives a chance to the ISP to correct failures in service delivery. Ticket close surveys are a great way to monitor processes throughout the user life-cycle.

- Interviews - Interviews allow the ISPs to get in-depth data on a situation through discussions with a specific user. The back-and-forth communication allows the interviewer to dig further into a specific area if required or skip topics that are not relevant. It typically provides a richness of information that would be difficult to achieve through surveys. The downside is the difficulty in measuring the feedback and the effort required.

- Focus groups - Focus groups are a great way to obtain more data about specific issues or initiatives. It allows the users to voice their opinion or ideas in a less-structured format than a survey. It also allows them to interact with one another and highlight issues they might not have come up with on their own. The downside is that focus groups, like interviews, don't provide data that is easily measurable.

The most common method to measure user satisfaction is a survey. Web-based surveys are cheap and easy to administer. There are plenty of providers that are happy to deliver the service or ISPs can do it themselves if they have the skills and competencies available internally. Modern tools allow survey customization based on the type of users and their responses. So if users say they are dissatisfied, other questions can be triggered to investigate the causes of dissatisfaction. This level of customization helps ISPs diagnose problems with their services and fix issues as they come up.

But users hate filling out surveys, don't they? Turns out this is not the case. 97% of users don't mind responding to surveys sent by their internal service providers. In fact, they see it as a sign that their opinion is important and valued.

Challenges of running surveys
Roughly 50% of internal service providers routinely measure user satisfaction. We would thus expect the industry to have a massive amount of satisfaction data to analyze, compare and benchmark. But that's not the case.

The problem with satisfaction is that organizations don't always follow a standard protocol for measuring satisfaction. Therefore it is impossible to compare apples-to-apples with other companies. Some will measure satisfaction on a 4 point scale, others on 7 points. Some will use industry standard questionnaires while others will make up their own questions.

I might have Photoshop installed on my computer, but this doesn't make me a graphic designer. Having the tools to measure satisfaction is not sufficient to make surveys valid. Satisfaction surveys require a thorough understanding of the biases that can occur in surveys, knowledge of statistical techniques, and subject matter expertise to apply the results in the context required.

Measuring satisfaction using an external partner isn't very expensive and allows comparisons with other organizations. (full disclosure: my company offers this service, so yes I might be a little biased). At the very least, an ISP that runs user satisfaction surveys should keep the survey questions and scales consistent from one survey to another so it can benchmark to itself over time.

What about Net Promoter Score?

In the recent years, a new metric has started appearing for measuring customer satisfaction: Net Promoter Score (NPS). The metric was developed and made popular by Fred Reichheld in his book "The Ultimate Question." The intent of the Net Promoter Score is to measure the loyalty that exists between a consumer and the provider by asking one simple question: How likely are you to recommend our company/product/service to your friends and colleagues? Respondents that rate this question low are labeled detractors, people that would actively undermine the brand. People that rate the question high are promoters, people that would actively recommend the brand.

The popularity of the approach has led to different attempts to replicate it in an internal service provider environment. But there are a few problems with this: internal service providers are a monopoly, accessible only to the organization's employees. Asking users if they would recommend their legal department to their family doesn't make much sense and can leave survey respondents clueless as to what kind of answer to provide.

Regardless, the metric has been adapted over time and while it isn't as meaningful for internal service providers, it is still useful since most business leaders are familiar with its definition and can use this score in their own operations. And it is a good way to demonstrate that you are holding yourself to the same standards as everyone else.

Misconceptions about user satisfaction

Some ISPs have a bad opinion about satisfaction surveys. Some even believe that users will never be satisfied, that it is impossible to meet all of their needs. Let's review the three most common myths about user satisfaction.

User satisfaction is expensive

The typical concern I hear when I talk about user satisfaction to IT leaders is, "The users want everything, and keeping them satisfied will cost us a fortune! We don't have that kind of money!"

We've seen from research that there is no correlation between ISP budgets and user satisfaction. So it is not how much money an organization spends that matters, but how it delivers its services. In fact, we will see throughout this book that the factors influencing user satisfaction have little to do with money. Attitude and communication are much more important.

User satisfaction also provides cost-saving opportunities. Users that are satisfied tend to accept changes, increasing the chances of project success and decreasing the need for change management (well, making change management easier and cheaper, if not eliminating it). Satisfied users are also more productive with their services and will tend to explore and learn much more than dissatisfied users. Finally, users that are satisfied tend to resolve problems themselves more, reducing the number of calls to the help-desk and making those calls easier and faster to resolve.

User satisfaction is about bending over backwards

Another concern I hear all the time is, "The users will hold us hostage, we won't be able to do anything that will have an impact on satisfaction like putting in a new system, because it will make our score go down!" or "We'll have to respond to small requests and bend over backward to meet all the needs of the users. I might as well hold their mouse for them!"

It seems some people confuse keeping users satisfied with the inability to say no. If you go to an ice cream shop and ask for a hamburger, it would be ridiculous to think they would serve one to you. As a customer, you wouldn't have those expectations since the menu is pretty clear about what they serve. The same is true with ISPs. If your catalog is clear about what you will and will not do, then it becomes a lot easier to say, "No, we're sorry but we cannot do this at this time. Could you use something on our menu instead?"

User satisfaction is about surveys

"Yes we take user satisfaction very seriously; we do a survey once a year!" The survey process is one of the ways organizations measure satisfaction, but not the only one. ISPs dedicated to user satisfaction will integrate discussions about service in their day-to-day activities. Managers will work with employees to evaluate their service skills and competencies and work with employees to improve them over time. They will solicit feedback from users when something isn't resolved to their satisfaction, and the ISP will work hard to correct any processes that make things difficult for the users. Satisfaction is about having a constant preoccupation with what being a user is like.

I know a CIO that kept talking about user satisfaction and how important it was to get it right. But whenever he had a problem with his computer, he would get his secretary to deal with it. She would call the help-desk and of course a team of technicians would arrive right away to fix the issue. The CIO lost a great opportunity to see for himself what the user experience is. Had he called the help-desk himself and insisted people follow the normal service call process, he would then have been able to see what the service was really like.

A balancing act

We've seen how important it is to balance the service delivered and the service expected in order to manage satisfaction. Now we'll see how expectations are actually formed.

The role of Expectations

Expectations in marriage

Nowhere in life are we lying more than when we are meeting someone. We dress nice, our hair is put together, and we keep our body noises to a minimum. We try to represent the best part of ourselves to the other person. And they do the same. Researchers would say we are presenting a limited, perhaps false version of ourselves, but the majority of people call it dating.

And we do all this for one good reason: competition. There are a lot of suitors out there who are after a mate. And there are lots of choices. Go to a dating site and you'll see large numbers of people who are available and looking. We need to distinguish ourselves from the pack and it is certainly not by showing our daily, no make-up, unshaven selves that we will achieve this.

This desire to weed out competition has a nasty side effect: it raises expectations from potential partners. No one is naive enough to think that you will always look this good and be this well-behaved. But they do expect a somewhat similar version of the person you were representing. They certainly were not expecting the old "bait and switch."

And it is these expectations that will help us decide if we want to spend the rest of our lives with someone. We have expectations about their looks, their attitude, their behaviour, their future potential abilities to raise a family, to be a good partner, to be supportive, etc. We develop expectations not only on what they are today but also on what they will become.

But what happens when these expectations turn out to be too high? A study by McNulty, J.K. and Karney investigated the impact of expectations on marriage. Their study attempted to answer a critical question: is it better to go into a marriage with low expectations or with high expectations?

There are benefits to having low expectations in a marriage (as there is anywhere). The chances of being disappointed are much lower, since if we don't expect our spouse to be a great partner, we are not surprised when it turns out that it is actually the case. Having high expectations only makes the disappointment that much greater when a spouse doesn't live up to their "advertised self." Since we know satisfaction is the difference between the expected service and the actual service, someone with high expectations of their spouse has a greater chance of being dissatisfied with their "service."

On the other hand, having low expectations for someone often results in service that lowers to match expectations. There is an old truism that says, "People will deliver what is expected of them". So if you expect the best, they are more likely to deliver the best.

The study followed 82 couples over four years to see which of the two scenarios was better. The couples participated in a three-hour interview where they filled in questionnaires and discussed a particularly contentious topic, all while being filmed. Subsequently, they would receive a questionnaire every six months and be brought back to the lab after two years for another round of interviews and questionnaire.

Over the four-year period, 17 couples were no longer couples; we can guess that expectations played a major role. With the other couples there was an interesting effect.

The couples that had started with high expectations had two different results. Some high expectation couples were greatly disappointed. Their high expectations were not met by their partners and they were dissatisfied with the outcome. They felt they were victims of the "bait and switch" or the "not exactly as advertised."

The second group with high expectations saw their expectations met. Their partners lived up to their expectations over time and their expectations served as an aspirational objective for both of them. If my partner expects me to be a great father, that expectation will likely motivate me to become a great father. We all love to meet the expectations of our loved ones. These couples blamed any partner shortcomings on external factors such as "He's stressed at work," "The kids are difficult," etc.

The low expectations couples saw more stable levels of satisfaction. Perhaps we could have expected for some of them to be "delighted," pleasantly surprised when their partners over-delivered on their promise. Surprisingly, this didn't happen. Low expectation spouses tended to achieve the level of expectation that was expected of them. This could be due to one of two reasons. Either the spouses were really good at assessing the potential of their spouse, or they couldn't recognize when their spouse was indeed over-delivering.

These results bring up an interesting idea concerning expectations. Having expectations that are too high can be detrimental, since it will be nearly impossible for others to consistently meet these high standards. However, having expectations that are too low will make exceptional performance almost meaningless, since it may not be recognized.

Under-promise, over-deliver?
My managers have always told me to under-promise and over-

deliver. This was their mantra for successful client relationships. But based on our marriage example, does it hold true?

Let's look at a business example: expectations for an IT project.

A study by Staples, Wong and Seddon showed the effect of expectations in IT projects. Intuitively we all know that high expectations can impact satisfaction. But they went one step further and investigated the effect of expectations in both directions: too high and too low. And what they found was pretty interesting.

As expected, having expectations that are too high resulted in users being dissatisfied. Again, this makes a lot of sense intuitively. If these users were expecting a system that is blazingly fast, easy to use and easy to learn, they were disappointed.

However, when expectations were too low, users were equally as disappointed. That seems counter-intuitive to everything we know about satisfaction. How could users be disappointed if they've received more than what was expected?

The findings seem to say that the most important factor is not whether the service is higher or lower than expected, but instead that the service is different. The variation between the service expected and the service delivered is the cause of dissatisfaction in those whose expectations were too high and too low.

Therefore, satisfaction is actually closer to a bell curve than a straight line. Satisfaction is maximized when what is delivered is exactly what is promised, but it starts to decline when what is delivered doesn't match what was promised.

How can we explain this effect? There are a few ways to look at this. The first is that the low expectations users pre-judge the capabilities of the system, regardless of what the system actually did once it was operating. This is similar to someone being told they will eat raw fish and subsequently finding the taste awful. Setting expectations low has led the user to actually form their opinion without even trying it. However, if the same fish is presented as a tasty, delicious meal called sushi that other people love, it will be considered more palatable.

The second effect could be that users do not accept low expectations. This is similar to teenagers buying a first car--they will buy a good-looking lemon, despite the fact their parents tell them that it is a bad idea. Teenagers refuse to think that such a beautiful car could represent thousands of dollars of problems in the future (and I speak from personal experience).

The trap
Another dangerous aspect of under-promising and over-delivering is that it labels you as a liar. Not an evil liar, mind you, but a liar nonetheless. The next time you promise something to users, they will tell themselves, "Oh well, he's telling me it will be ok, but I know he really means it will be blazing fast and serve coffee. He's always too conservative." And users will thus set their expectations accordingly.

This creates a situation where the opposite effect is created. By trying to manage expectations to set them at a realistic level and give ourselves a chance to meet and exceed them, we have actually inflated expectations to a level we don't know if we can reach, levels that might very well be unrealistic.

Right on the money should be the way to go
So what is the solution? Of course, it is to promise and deliver exactly the same thing.

By aiming for the top of the bell curve, we ensure that expectations will match exactly what will be delivered and users will not be surprised either way.

This is one of the reasons why user involvement in projects is the main factor that influences satisfaction. It allows users to set their expectations on exactly what will be delivered, to the point where they will be able to test it, have a slight influence on direction and know exactly what will be delivered. Expectations are formed based on their own interaction, instead of what was promised by the ISP.

How we form expectations

Expectations come from various places. We'll see here the three main sources that influence users' expectations: what was promised, what others received, and prior experience.

What was promised

When we enter into a service relationship, we do so based on a promise. Sometimes that promise is very formal through a contract or a service level agreement, while other times it is based on intangibles like the atmosphere or the price. These elements help us form a set of expectations when we have nothing else to base expectations on. Seeing a brochure for a nice hotel in the Caribbean, we see the endless array of empty beach chairs. We see a single couple in the deep blue pool smiling and looking at each other passionately. This kind of image helps us form our expectations for what our vacations will be like.

Unfortunately, these promises don't always turn out to be true. When you get to the hotel, you realize that you have to wake-up at 7:00 am to reserve a beach chair or else they will all be taken. The pool is crowded with kids playing and the bar is full of very loud people smoking and generally being rude. Quite a difference from the brochure.

But to be fair, the brochure never said the hotel would be empty. All it did is show the facilities. You, as a user of that hotel, created expectations of what the experience would be like. And a simple search on Google would probably have told you the truth before you went.

This is why when trying to set expectations, it is important not only to describe what users will receive, but also what they will NOT receive. Although this is a lot less sexy when advertising it is critical.

What others received

We tend to trust our friends and family much more than advertisers, which is probably a good thing. Going back to our example of the hotel, if we know people who went there last year, we will ask about their experience and adjust our own expectations accordingly. As a potential user, we tend to feel that our friends' experiences are not only more credible (after all, they have nothing to gain) but also closer to our own attitudes. If they liked it, chances are we will like it too.

In an ISP context, users get their information from other users, either by soliciting it directly, "Hey, how did it work the last time they upgraded your computer?" or by hearing about it through the grapevine (most commonly known as complaining). These pieces of information will help a user that has never dealt with you form an opinion of your ability as a service provider and adjust their expectations accordingly.

Prior experience

How many times have you been in a meeting, talking about an aspect of your company that is problematic, and one of your colleagues says, "Where I came from, we used to be really good at doing this." And then he goes on and on about how his previous employer was better at every aspect of the business, to a point you think, "Why did you leave then?"

Of course, everyone comes with prior baggage and experiences. These experiences play an important role in shaping expectations. If an employee had worked for a big company with a very mature IT department, they will be surprised and disappointed when they start working for a small or medium business with only one tech support guy who also maintains the web site. Their expectations had been set on various aspects of service delivery in terms of rapidity, competencies, attitude, etc.

The same thing applies for your own company. A user that has interacted with your ISP several times has come to expect a certain level of service based on what they received in the past. These past experiences represent the most important aspect of user expectations.

You've probably been to McDonalds more times than you care to admit. So, chances are you have a very good idea of what the experience will be like the next time you go there. Long lines, a cashier that speaks too quickly to understand, and having a hard time finding a table. Yet you also know it will be fast, have a consistent taste and the place will be clean.

Now, McDonalds might try to advertise that they are like a Parisian Cafe, offering gourmet coffees and a nice ambiance with nice decorations and fireplaces. But deep down you know it will be the same old McDonalds with long lines.

Prior experience is so strong that it takes a lot of advertising or peer recommendations to offset. If you've been dissatisfied in the past, chances are no amount of advertising will persuade you to go back.

How they all influence satisfaction
The combination of these sources helps us form our expectations for a given service.

Left unmanaged, these expectations tend to grow out of control. People are typically overly optimistic, seeing only the positive in what is presented, forgetting about the less pleasurable elements. We also tend to solicit the feedback of our friends who tend to be overly enthusiastic or very negative, but seldom balanced. Finally, if our experiences with a service are good, we tend to increase our expectations over time.

Managing (dis) satisfaction

Now that we know what it takes to satisfy users, there are no reasons to have dissatisfied users, right? Well, not quite. In the next section we will see some of the common reasons why users are not happy with the services they are receiving.

Why are your users dissatisfied?

Creating dissatisfaction

Back when I was a CIO, occasionally I would get a call from an angry user.

One such experience was a Monday morning, and the user had called me on my cell while I was driving to work. The receptionist at our headquarters office had tremendous problems with her computer and was very vocal about it, to whoever would listen.

So the first thing I did when I got to the office was to check the system to see what steps had been taken to resolve her computer issues. Sure enough, more memory had been added but it wasn't an old computer, less than 2 years old. It had a good setup, a solid image, and we had never had problems with this configuration in the past. The technicians' notes showed that the computer was responsive and working well. So what was wrong with it?

Her office was right on the other side of the street so I decided to go and check it out for myself. When I walked into her department it became apparent to me what the problem was. She was the only employee with only one screen. Everyone else was using our newer setup with two monitors that we had deployed for the new ERP system. Mind you, she wasn't a user of the ERP, so she technically didn't really need the new setup, so she was left with her older but still very good machine.

Once I started digging into the problem with her, we quickly came to the conclusion that the computer was working well and had no real issues. The problem was jealousy. Everyone else had two screens and she only had one.

Actually, it wouldn't be fair to call it jealousy. It was unfairness. She felt she wasn't treated to the same privileges as everyone else. We had created a dissatisfied user not by delivering poor service, but by giving better service to everyone else around her.

Satisfaction is relative

As we've seen, satisfaction is a very relative thing. Users can be satisfied or dissatisfied for a variety of reasons. And even worse, some users might be very satisfied while others are very dissatisfied with the exact same service at the same time.

The most important component of satisfaction we've seen is expectation. Users have a predetermined view on how service should be provided and when reality doesn't match expectations, then they are dissatisfied.

In this section we will look at the most common causes of dissatisfaction. We will see that communication is a critical element of setting and managing expectations with users. We will also see how being a monopoly puts you at a disadvantage when dealing with users, and how stress and fairness can have a significant impact on user satisfaction.

One for you, two for me?

The Ultimatum Game was often used in economics and psychology. Two participants were to split 10$. The twist is that the participants were in different rooms and the first participant decided how much money he wanted to give the second participant. But the second participant could refuse the deal, in which case both participants ended up with nothing. For example, Participant A was given 10$. Participant A decided to keep 7$ and give 3$ to the person in the other room; they don't know each other and will never meet. The second person could accept or refuse the deal in which case both participants would get nothing.

What is most interesting is that economic theories would say that the first person should act in his own self-interest and keep the maximum of the money, say 9$. Again, economic theories predict that the second person should take whatever they can get, say the remaining 1$. This split would be in the best interests of both people. The first person would get as much as possible out of the deal and the second person would get something, which is still better than nothing.

But this is where economic theories fail. What the study found is that the second participant in most cases would rather punish the bad deal by refusing it, even if both participants ended up with nothing. Thus the second participant would rather lose the free dollar if the first participant gets the biggest share of the money. Why would someone prefer to get nothing, just to see the other person not win? Well, it goes back to the principle of fairness.

Fairness is an important element of our expectations. According to Oliver and Swann, a customer needs to be treated fairly to feel satisfied.

Let's go back to our earlier coffee example. You go in a coffee shop and expect fast, courteous service, hot coffee and a fair price. These are your expectations. If the coffee place can provide that to you, then in theory you would be satisfied. Yet, if the customer in front of you gets a free donut and you don't get one, then you would probably be dissatisfied. Why? The donut wasn't even on your list of criteria. Perhaps you don't even like donuts. Yet, because the other customer got something you didn't, suddenly your level of satisfaction dropped. The same would be true if the cashier smiled and made small talk to the person in front of you but didn't talk to you. You would feel cheated, as if you didn't get something you deserved.

Now imagine how this applies to an ISP. Over and over I've seen the level of service vary depending if you knew the people in support, if you were located at headquarters or in satellite offices, if you were an executive, close to an executive, or simply a clerk. Who gets the new computers in your company? Did the company deploy iPads? Who got them first? Any preferential treatment can backfire by appearing unfair to the other users.

Now imagine if you were on the receiving end of the unfair transaction. Your colleague got a brand new laptop, ultra-light and glossy with a huge hard drive while you're still walking around with your antique pc that weighs eight pounds and takes a full coffee break to start-up. No amount of courtesy and support would make up for the difference in computers with your colleague. Every time you boot up the monster you would think of your colleague who can simply open the lid and get to work. Every time the straps dig in your shoulder when you travel you would think of your colleague who barely feels it. In other words, your satisfaction would plummet.

Strangely, this would probably not happen nearly as much if everyone had the old, bulky laptops. Fairness would be restored and the service would be judged on initial expectations only, not on new expectations created by the colleague or by IT.

How does this apply to everyday situations? Although we've talked about it already, consistency is key. Nothing kills satisfaction more quickly than having variations in service delivery.

But, does it make sense to have preferential treatment? Yes, definitely. But the trick is to be open and up-front about it. It is ok to have a VIP service as long as the service is acknowledged, and that service levels are well defined. Like anything else, consistency is key.

Simply being friends with someone in IT is not a sufficient reason to get better service.

Victim of the Stockholm syndrome?

I had just finished running a user satisfaction survey for one of my clients and the results were actually pretty good. Users were generally satisfied with the services provided and liked the responsiveness of the team. The manager was a little bit incredulous of the results. His first reaction was, "Maybe they are victims of the Stockholm syndrome."

If you are not familiar with the Stockholm syndrome, it happens when kidnapping victims develop a bond with their kidnappers, often going so far as protecting them and at times forming strong emotional bonds.

His attitude was right, though. Users often feel like hostages. They have a job to do and they have to do it despite the ISP's best efforts to sabotage them.

We were on a cruise and my wife was out of sunscreen lotion. No big deal, we decided to just head to the cruise shop and buy some. Of course the shop had outrageously priced bottles of sunscreen. How can these people sleep at night charging so much for a little bottle of sunscreen? We were outraged. This is taking advantage of people that don't have a choice, since there were no other stores on the boat. So our choice was simple, buy it or do without. So of course we bought it, although we were very displeased. In fact, we were clearly dissatisfied. Even when using the product we couldn't stop talking about how much we paid for it. We were outraged.

When we got home from the cruise, my wife went to the store to buy some more sunscreen. There were shelves full of the stuff, different brands and size. She ended up buying the same thing for about the same price. The cruise store wasn't so expensive after all. We laughed. In fact, there were items we remembered from the cruise store that were cheaper than at the grocery store. So why were we so dissatisfied? We felt hostage. There was no choice, no competition. It was a monopoly.

The same with ISPs. Users don't have a choice about whether to use your services or not. No one else offers them IT services, accounting services or HR services. They must use what is provided or do without. And in some cases they can't do without, they are obligated to use the services.

This is compounded by the fact that most users are also buyers of services in their personal lives. They see new iPhones come out, they purchase computers and laptops for home, they perhaps already have brand preferences. So when we dictate a choice of technology and the tools they must use, they feel taken hostage. That can be even more compounded by the guardian role that the ISP often plays. They may say, "If you want access to this information you need to justify your need and get three signatures." Or "No, we don't believe you need a tablet computer," even if you travel constantly and using a laptop on a plane is a huge inconvenience.

Studies show that when dissatisfied with a service, 88% of consumers simply change providers. Thus, the first reaction of people who are dissatisfied is to look for alternatives. It is simply easier to vote with our feet, walking away and finding a new supplier.

Monopolies go against the first reaction of the 88% of dissatisfied users. They cannot vote with their feet. So what are the options available to them? They may complain to each other, talk to their boss about it, but most likely they will simply remain dissatisfied without telling anyone. These users will slowly stop using your service to the extent they can. How many rogue users do we see in organizations? People who are buying their own software or using web applications without involving ISPs? This is a reaction to the monopoly nature where the user's reaction is simply to say, "They will probably just get in the way, so why involve them?"

ISPs and anxiety

We sometimes forget that business users may or may not have the same comfort level with ISP's solutions that we have. The users come from a variety of backgrounds and may be highly specialized in various areas, but most likely your particular trade is not one of them.

If you've tried helping a family member with their computer then you may understand what is meant by techno-stress.

When I was in university, I trained people on how to use MS Office. These were very basic classes where I taught skills like writing a letter in Word, doing a budget in Excel or doing a small presentation in PowerPoint. These classes were typically for older people who had just gotten a computer and wanted to get better at using it.

One student asked how to open a file. He kept dragging it instead of clicking it. So I tell him to double-click on the file he wants to open. No success. He tells me again that it doesn't work and this time I make my way over to his workstation to see exactly what was happening. The gentleman was doing everything right, except he waited 3-4 seconds between clicks. So I explained to him that he needed to click a little bit faster. His answer to me was "With the amount of money I'm paying for this thing, it can't even wait for me?"

While teaching I was shocked by the number of people that were simply afraid of touching computers. Several people would physically step back a few inches every time they were done with a task. A few wouldn't keep their hand on the mouse. You could sense they had some fear and apprehension toward the machine.

Techno-stress exists at many levels. Perhaps no one is physically afraid of computers in your organization, but chances are that there are people who are less than comfortable with them. I've seen people going to meetings with both their laptop and their calculator. And since most ISPs now deliver their services through some form of computer program, that can quickly become problematic.

Factors that create techno-stress

There are five factors that generate techno-stress for end-users. The first one is techno-overload that occurs when users are forced to work faster or work longer hours because of technology. This typically happens when new systems are deployed and processes are not explained, reviewed or simplified. Take the example of a CRM system being deployed within an organization. If the sales people keep doing what they have been doing but now have to do more administrative work, more work has been created for them. Therefore their workload has increased overnight simply by adding new technology.

The second cause of techno-stress is called techno-invasion. Many people cannot live without their BlackBerry or iPhone anymore. And that is actually a problem. Technology (especially mobile technologies) have encroached on the personal lives of people and left them feeling that they are always "on", that they never have any downtime, and that they should be checking their email at all times, day and night.

The third cause of techno-stress is techno-complexity. Chances are your users are very good at what they do. They may be highly skilled people and have many years of experience in their fields. They probably consider themselves as very competent. But overnight, we throw a new system at them, and now they have a hard time simply doing their work. What used to be easy for them is now complicated, time-consuming and inefficient. This new complexity makes users feel inadequate and incompetent doing something they used to excel at.

The fourth cause of techno-stress is techno-insecurity. When deploying new services jobs change, and organizations try to use the technology to increase productivity, and this often happens by downsizing. Therefore, users are left wondering if the success of a new system will result in loss of employment.

Finally, the fifth cause of techno-stress is techno-uncertainty. Just when a user finally starts to understand how the system works, we upgrade it or change it. The users are thus continually wondering when they will have to be retrained again in order to keep doing their day-to-day work.

Impact of stress

The biggest impact that these stressors have on users are diminished performance. The combination of new technologies, demands on their existing work, and the pressures to produce benefits from the new system by increasing productivity, often cause the exact opposite effect. Users become less competent in their work and worse, they realize this impact will create further anxiety.

This diminished performance and increased anxiety have a direct impact on their satisfaction. They now perceive the technology as being a hindrance rather than a help. Of course, this situation can be temporary, simply the time it takes for users to go through the "learning curve." But it can also become permanent if the speed of the change and the impact on users are not managed.

This is not to say that change is bad and should be avoided. Later we will see how communication and user involvement (even passive user involvement) can help alleviate stressors and help improve user satisfaction with new service deployment.

Complaint and service recovery

In the service industry there is an adage: a complaint is a gift from the gods. The reality is that very few people complain (only 4%). This means that for every complaint you get, there are 24 people that are dissatisfied but won't tell you.

There are many reasons not to complain:

- First, it takes courage to complain. Making a complaint might result in a discussion or even a confrontation.
- Second, most people feel that complaining won't make a difference. "Sure I can complain, but is anyone listening? They'll keep doing the same old thing."
- And third, putting in a complaint requires people to articulate exactly what they want, something that is not always easy to do, especially in an environment that is complex.
- And finally, users are worried about retaliation. "If I log a complaint, the help-desk person will be reprimanded and then he will be mad at me. I might never get good service afterwards."

As a client, why should I bother with this? I've seen many ISPs but few had a way for users to log a complaint. The one excuse for this is "The users just have to call the service-desk back to tell them the issue is not fixed." Right. But the complaint could be in many areas not directly related to the service-desk. How can a user tell you that they are dissatisfied with the service-desk person's attitude? Or that the wait time was too long? Or that the skill set of the agent isn't good enough?

When I was a CIO I encouraged people to email or call me directly when they had complaints. My email and cell phone were on all the communications sent out and on the user support portal. At first my staff was worried I'd be overwhelmed with emails. But in reality I only got one or two per week. And those emails or calls allowed me to talk to users, understand the situation and really get to the root of the issue. I would then make sure the user's problem was fixed, but also that the root cause was addressed and resolved.

Service recovery is a critical part of any service organization. Getting the complaint is only half the battle. The second half is to make sure the complaint is handled appropriately and the situation corrected.

There is nothing worse than a complaint that ends up going nowhere. This is like a second slap in the face. "Not only is their service poor, they don't even respond to their complaints!" Service recovery isn't difficult. You correct the problem and then follow-up with the user to make sure the problem was indeed fixed to their satisfaction. Then you explain how you will make sure that the situation will not repeat itself. But too few ISPs do this today.

Delivering amazing value

Of course, not everyone will do things the same way to meet the needs of their clients. After all, there is no one way to deliver amazing value. That's where the personality profiles comes in.

The Accountant, The Butler, the Nanny and the Agent. Each personality is a world unto itself, each with their own traits, strengths and weaknesses. Once we identify the two main dimensions that define the personalities, you'll see that some ISPs are more directive, why some are better at serving their users and most importantly, that there is no best personality. The best personality is the one that fits with what the organization needs.

Part 2. The ISP Personality Profiles

Meet the four personality profiles: the Accountant, the Butler, the Nanny and the Agent.

When I'm out shopping, I'm always surprised how companies treat their customers. Major retailers rely on their customers to browse through aisles and find what they are looking for by themselves. Small boutiques rely on young salespeople to "guide" you toward their most expensive clothes and shoes. And high-end electronic stores will bombard you with technical specifications that most people don't understand, including the sales people. All of these stores offer a different experience to their customers and yet, everyone seems pretty happy about it.

Working as a consultant for Gartner, I was privileged to work with many different internal service providers. And each provider had a different relationship with its users. Some were confrontational while some were friendly. Some ISPs seemed to have limitless budgets while others had to scavenge old parts to fix their aging equipment.

But despite these differences, there was no common element that would predict their relationship with the business.

It's not just about the service

One client offered a very interesting problem. The ISP was very focused on delivering great service. The ISP staff would work tirelessly to quickly answer user requests, and to provide whatever users wanted. They would rarely say no, always find ways to make things happen and would consistently deliver as promised. In fact, it was one of the few ISPs that I've met that had achieved a level of service this high.

Yet, their users were dissatisfied. They thought their ISP didn't get it, that it wasn't a good partner. The staff of the ISP was discouraged and burned-out, feeling that whatever they did wouldn't be enough. The ISP leader kept asking more and more from its staff. But nothing worked.

They brought us in to see how they compared with other providers. The leader believed that they were above and beyond everyone else in terms of service, and that there was no way users could really expect more than what they were providing. After doing our initial assessment, it was clear that they were indeed above and beyond everyone else in their industry.

But a funny thing happened when we started interviewing some of their users and clients. The users commented over and over again how they thought that the ISP was too reactive. Yes, it delivered great service but all they did was extinguish fires. And yes, they agreed to almost anything, but now they were stuck with customer information across several different systems, making it difficult to get a complete view of their customers. They would have preferred that the ISP inform them that his was going to happen, before they invested hundreds of thousands of dollars in several new systems.

The ISP delivered everything they wanted, but only that. What users needed instead was a partner that could help them make the right decisions and prevent issues from happening in the first place.

Partnerships are built from both service and business orientation

It became clear rapidly that successful ISPs were not only good at delivering services, they were also closely aligned to the needs of the company.

Luckily, the business literature already had two concepts to explain these ideas:

- Service orientation: Service orientation represents the focus on customer service the ISP has. Some companies manage ISP as cost centres and try to minimize interactions with users, while others try to be ultra-responsive to users' needs.
- Business orientation: Business orientation measures the level of influence the ISP has on the business. Some ISPs are simply focused on commodity services, while others have a deep understanding of business issues and propose solutions to address them.

Each of these dimensions work on a scale, which will be defined in the next chapter.

The personality profiles

Together, the service and business orientations makes up four personality profiles:

- The Accountant: Intense focus on cost control above all else.
- **The Butler:** Lives to serve, wants to satisfy its users at all costs.
- **The Nanny:** Knows what's good for the company and will do whatever it takes.
- **The Agent:** One step ahead of everyone else, she is the next CEO.

These aren't black or white personality classifications. An internal service provider might belong to more than one family depending on the service or circumstances. But, we've found that it is a simple and useful framework to classify internal service providers and predict the alignment it will have with the organization.

The instruction manual for the personality profiles

Once you understand the role that service and business orientation plays on the daily behaviour of ISP staff, you'll realize how we can predict the role and value the ISP will have in the organization. To begin, below is a snapshot preview. In this chart you'll see the definition of each personality profile, and each profile's main characteristics.

	Service orientation	Business Orientation	Description	Example
Accountant	Low	Low	Manages its budget tightly.	Walmart
Butler	High	Low	Lives to serve.	Starbucks
Nanny	Low	High	Knows what's good for you.	Apple
Agent	High	High	Enables users.	Weight Watchers

Each personality has a different perspective on their role in the organization and the way they should serve users. The Butlers will provide a high-touch service, bending over backward to serve their users, while Nannies will dictate orientations and methods to their users.

It would be easy to say that the Agent is the best of all, but as we'll see in the following pages, each profile has advantages and challenges. But first, let's look at what we mean by service and business orientation.

Service orientation

Recognizing good service

We all know when we are getting good service. At the store, restaurant or movie theatre you instantly recognize excellent customer service. It's often not about the tools (although it helps) or the procedures. What really makes great customer service is the person's attitude. When you get great service, you feel like the other person genuinely cares about you, that they really want to create a good experience for you.

Employees that provide great customer service are engaged, welcoming, and alert to your needs. They work long hours, but they seem to genuinely appreciate their job and how they can help others. Attitude is very important. But attitude is not enough, it must be nurtured and rewarded across a company. It is easy to crush a good attitude if the boss only cares about productivity.

What interests my boss fascinates me

Perhaps you remember starting a new job. Despite your education and experience, you don't really know how to behave at first. What should you wear? You don't want to be better dressed than your boss, but you don't want to look like a slob either. Are meetings casual or very formal? Is it ok to disagree with your boss in public?

These are all of the non-written rules that make up the norms in your organization. And these norms drive behaviour. People instinctively pick up on these norms and adjust their behaviour in order to fit in. Altogether these norms make up the culture of the organization.

Some cultures encourage a customer service approach in their daily behaviours while some seem to almost discourage it.

Service orientation is defined by the employee's perceptions of the practices, procedures, and behaviours that are expected and get rewarded and supported, with regard to user service and user service quality.

Keeping a high service orientation is not easy. It requires a daily preoccupation with doing what's right for users. Some leaders say they are customer-focused, but only when they do their annual satisfaction survey. The rest of the time, they are focused on cost control.

Employees pick up on these cues and adapt their behaviour accordingly. Whatever interests my boss will most likely fascinate me. On the other hand, if my boss never talks about customer service, chances are it will fade in importance for me.

What drives a service culture?

Good service doesn't happen by accident. Hiring employees with the right attitude is only a start. The culture of the organization must also promote user service in everything.

Research has defined six critical factors that influence the service orientation of an internal service provider:

- **Service leadership and vision:** The extent to which the ISP managers take action to guide and reward the delivery of quality service, such as goal setting, work planning, and coordination, recognition and rewards.
- **Service quality:** The extent to which ISP professionals give

prompt, professional service to their users.

- **Customer feedback:** The extent to which client feedback regarding service quality is solicited and addressed.
- **Customer communications:** The extent to which the ISP professionals openly and frequently communicate with customers regarding task-related issues.
- **Physical proximity:** The extent at which the ISP professionals are located closely to their clients. Adjoining offices: same floor in the same building, different floor in the same building, different building in the same city, different city.
- **Coworker support:** The extent to which the ISP professionals work together to get the job done.

By measuring the level of each of these six factors it is possible to quantitatively evaluate the service orientation of an internal service provider.

Low service orientation: Getting work done despite the users

Perhaps you've seen this. You call an internal service provider and the person responding sounds like you just interrupted them while they are doing something important. He seems annoyed to have to deal with you. You begin to explain your problem and without having the time to finish, he tells you that it's an easy problem. He asks you to try some specific instructions, but he says it so quickly you don't have the time to write it down. He asks to call back if it doesn't work and then hangs up, barely leaving you enough time to say good-bye.

You try the instructions, but of course it doesn't work. Now you're stuck with two choices: call back and again feel like you're disrupting him, or live with the problem. Many people decide to live with the problem, but instead you call back. He then asks you some very specific questions you have no answer to. You then execute a few commands you don't understand, and then he declares the problem fixed. He goes on to tell you the problem was all your fault and next time, don't try to fix it yourself.

You leave the interaction exhausted, slightly confused and feeling bad. You'll probably think twice about calling next time.

A low orientation ISP has very little concern for its users. Not that it goes out of its way to deliver bad service, far from it. They want their users to be productive and efficient just as much as anyone else, but they realize that users don't have a choice, and feel they don't have to spend too much time and energy in managing the user experience.

For them, service is a cost that should be minimized. Whenever an ISP staff works on solving a problem, they are not creating value or moving projects forward.

When hiring, they tend to focus on skills more than attitude. They want someone that can do the job first and foremost. Then they'll worry about attitude if it becomes a problem. This makes ISP teams that are very competent but more concerned about their own work than serving users adequately.

High service orientation: My work is the users

When you call a high service orientation ISP it is a significantly different experience. After being greeted by a cheerful representative, you explain your problem at length, only being interrupted by thoughtful questions from the agent. He then proceeds to reassure you that he will work with you to get your problem resolved as soon as possible. He asks you a series of diagnostic questions that are worded in plain English, not in tech-filled jargon. He then tries a solution and stay on the line with you while you test the solution to see if it works.

He then asks you if there is anything else he can help you with, and genuinely means it. He may even ask you if he can take a look himself just to make sure everything else is in order, just so you'll avoid future problems. When you finally hang up, you get an email shortly after asking if you are happy with the service you provided. Of course you'll answer yes, since he was most helpful. But, if you answered no, his supervisor would immediately call you to find out what happened and get someone else to help you fix your problem right away, if necessary.

What happens if he can't resolve your problem immediately? The agent would give an estimate of when it will be completed, and continue to follow up with you regularly to inform you how your issue is evolving. He would call you even to say that nothing has changed, just to reassure you that they are still working on it. The high-service orientation ISP wants to make sure you know that they take service seriously, and communication is an important part of this.

A high-service orientation person is not interrupted when you call them, that's what they were waiting for. They build their entire department around supporting their users. They invest in tools and systems to be able to track user information and track issues so nothing falls through the crack. They perform regular user satisfaction surveys to make sure that their level of service is still adequate. And they think about user service every day, assigning themselves objectives and tracking results continuously. Serving users is their business.

But as we've seen, service orientation is only half of the equation. The other half, the business orientation, involves working hand-in-hand with the company to move it forward, which we'll see in the next chapter.

Business orientation

A few years ago there was a major trend for companies to outsource their internal service providers. They believed they could achieve significant cost savings by outsourcing to cheaper locations such as India or Pakistan. Their reasoning was pretty simple: ISPs are a cost centre that should be optimized. They don't really bring value since they are a commodity, thus it makes sense to get it at the lowest price possible.

Internal service providers started defending themselves by claiming that companies   would lose all of the business insights and partnerships the ISPs had accumulated, and that a cheap outsourcer would never be able to provide the same level of value.

This brought two reactions: the first one where business executives started thinking about the loss of such a strategic advantage and finding ways to optimize costs without outsourcing, or executives laughing at the idea that their ISP understood anything about the business the company is in.

Internal VS external

What differentiates internal suppliers is their keen understanding of the company and business and of how they can help it achieve its objectives. That knowledge, combined with a common willingness to succeed, is what drives company to use internal service providers instead of external suppliers.

But not every ISP really understands their company and its business. In fact some ISPs are no better than external suppliers. Some ISPs are perfectly happy simply delivering a service without really understanding how it is used and how the company benefits from it.

Business orientation is defined by the level of influence the ISP has on the company. It distinguishes providers that simply deliver a service without understanding the context from partners that use their skills and knowledge to move the business forward. At its extreme, high business orientation acts as the driver for change in a company, coming up with new ideas and initiatives to transform the business.

Maintaining a high business orientation is not simple. It requires mastering your own domain (IT, HR, finance, etc.) and understanding the specific industry your company is in. It also requires having the business acumen to understand how services will impact business units and how to best help them achieve their objectives.

This requires a different breed of employee; people comfortable having a foot in two different worlds and bridging them with their skills and insights. It also requires people that are comfortable speaking to company leaders in their own language and simplifying their department's concepts so they are understood.

More than just knowledge

Business orientation isn't simply understanding the company and business. If that was the case, then most ISPs would probably rate high already. High business orientation consists in using this knowledge to influence the company in the right direction, something much more difficult.

Research has identified six factors that contribute to a high business orientation:

- **Communication maturity:** Ensures ongoing knowledge sharing across the company and the understanding of business by the ISP and vice versa.
- **Competency / Value measurement maturity:** Demonstrates the value the ISP contributes to the business.
- **Governance maturity:** Ensures that the appropriate participants of the company and the ISP are reviewing the priorities and allocation of resources.
- **Partnership maturity:** Reflects the level of trust developed among participants of the ISP and the company in sharing risk and rewards.
- **Scope maturity:** Signifies the level of flexibility and transparency the ISP provides to business.
- **Skills maturity:** Reflects the level of innovation, change readiness, hiring and retaining, and how they are contributing to the overall organizational effectiveness.

Business orientation is measured by evaluating the level of maturity for each of these factors. The right combination of process, tools and people is required to rate high on the business orientation scale.

Paying the bills

Accounting departments are continually under pressure to reduce costs. To help with this mandate, most have automated the low-value, transactional processes that makes up their function, such as accounts payable.

The account payable team role is to make sure the company pays its suppliers on a timely basis while respecting the company's guidelines. For example, if a supplier gives you 30 days to pay the invoice, then it makes no sense paying it before it is due. That would be like refusing a no-interest loan. To facilitate these guidelines they've established systems and processes.

They've also started pushing a lot of their work to the users themselves. A new vendor is contracted? Please fill out the vendor creation form that contains all of the information required. Planning to buy something, please fill out a purchase order form with all of the accounting codes required. By pushing these tasks to the users they've been able to concentrate on the transactional aspect of their job, making them more efficient.

But this task displacement didn't take into account the huge workload that users already faced. While it used to be fairly straightforward to hire a consultant, now they have to create a new vendor record, create a PO, fill in all of the accounting information, receive the invoice and approve it. Only then would accounting process it for payment.

This made things very efficient for the internal service provider, but created headaches for their clients. While the ISP used to provide guidance and help in purchasing what was needed, now they have relegated themselves to the simple role of payment processor. Of course the next logical step for them is to outsource everything, since the low business orientation makes the department almost indistinguishable from an external service provider.

Better living through technology

Information technology (IT) departments used to be known for being geeks working isolated from the rest of the business. They could make sense of computers and were the gods of the enterprise systems. No major change in the company could happen without their involvement. IT understood its power and often yielded it, stopping initiatives because they didn't comply with "security guidelines", or forcing long, painful authorization processes for other initiatives. Overall, IT was perceived as a roadblock.

The market started reacting to this by creating software as a service solution (SaaS). SaaS is hosted at the providers' location and can be leased, paying a monthly fee instead of paying everything up front. It also didn't need IT's involvement. This created a deluge of departments that started to bypass IT and develop their own solution, using SaaS to support their initiatives.

This led to the introduction of a new wave of IT leaders, leaders much more astute at how the company operates and know how technology can be used to move the company forward. Leaders that were even willing to use these new solutions to speed up the deployment process.

These new leaders are much more preoccupied with the company than by the technology supporting it. However, they are willing to work with the business units to develop proof-of-concepts, tests, pilots and trials, something traditional IT leaders would have never accepted.

This trend also led to these leaders taking more important roles in their company. While traditional IT leaders used to report to finance, more and more started reporting to the CEO directly. They were often put in charge of not just technology but also business processes that cross departments and are difficult to manage.

Their high business orientation changed the IT department from a reactive organization that responded to requests, to a department leading transformational projects.

What happens when an ISP is low on both service and business orientation? It becomes an Accountant, a relentless machine driven by optimizing costs. You want your ISP to be lean and efficient? Call in the Accountants.

The Accountant

Walmart, the ultimate Accountant

Is there a place more boring than Walmart? I mean let's face it, I probably prefer going to the dentist more than going to Walmart. I actually dread the weekly visit.

The first thing you see when entering a Walmart is the greeter. The greeter is always smiling, welcoming. He or she will offer you a shopping cart to be helpful. But the reality is that the greeter is not there for you, the greeter is part of the loss prevention team, i.e. they are there to make sure you don't steal anything. Most retailers see a shrinkage (a fancy word for loss that includes theft) rate of around 1%, which can make a significant dent in profits, especially for a low margin retailer like Walmart. Greeters help prevent shrinkage.

But being a greeter can be a difficult job. One elderly greeter was punched in the face in Batavia, NY when she asked a customer to present a receipt for the purchases made. The poor 70-year-old woman had to be hospitalized.

Then you are hit with rows and rows of shelves. Everything at Walmart is designed to make shopping convenient, and by convenient they mean fast. Each Walmart typically has 3400 customers visit each store every day. There is a need to get those customers in and out of there fast, so the store doesn't become crowded. Walmart does that by having aisles large enough to accommodate multiple shopping carts, by having products in sufficient numbers that are conveniently located so they are easy to grab.

Walmart sells a little bit of everything, from food products to high-end televisions. But don't expect any help in deciding which product is best for you. Most Walmart employees are shelf stockers, they are there to replenish the inventory and make sure it is always available. If you are wondering if the television set you are looking at will be compatible with your home stereo, then you are out of luck. The best advice you'll hear is, "If it doesn't work simply bring it back for a refund!" And don't expect to have anyone offer to bring the TV to your car after buying it. If you need help you will have to ask and then wait until one of the "boys from the back of the store" shows up to help you.

When you are ready to check out, there are rows and rows of cashiers. After all, Walmart makes $36 Million in sales every hour. That's a lot of Tide boxes being scanned and bagged. But not all the cashiers are open, of course. Walmart monitors checkout wait times and makes sure that just the right number of checkouts is open to make the buying process smooth, at the minimum cost for the store.

And when you leave, the greeters are there again to check your receipt and make sure you paid for everything that's in your shopping cart. Walmart's anti-theft policy is simple: everyone is a suspect. Greeters systematically check receipts and bags of everyone, not just people acting suspicious.

Does that sound like a fantastic shopping experience to you? No, there is only one reason to go to Walmart: great prices. And considering that 42% of Walmart customers are families with a total income of less than $40,000 a year, price is important. Most of these families could care less about the harsh lighting, the real role of the greeters or the fact that you have to wait in line at the cashier. They want to get quality products for the lowest price possible. And Walmart delivers.

The entire culture of Walmart is designed to keep prices low. And that is apparent in everything they do.

For starters, being a supplier to Walmart is a difficult business. Walmart has very strict contracts in place to guarantee product availability, price and delivery. Suppliers are given delivery windows that are only 15 minutes wide. If they fail to deliver within this window, they are fined heavily. In fact, some suppliers I've talked to believe Walmart makes more profit from the penalties they place on suppliers than they do from selling their products (although I have a hard time believing that).

But suppliers are not the only ones being mistreated; employees are also getting the low-cost treatment. Lawsuits have erupted showing Walmart had asked employees to skip their break, and have an unpaid lunch. Or if an employee forgets to punch out at the end of the day, managers assume that the employee worked only one minute, denying them a full day of pay. Employees are routinely asked to work overtime for no pay, on their own time. Examples of employee mistreatment abound, from in-store employees to distribution, and even in their supply chain.

Employees are not the only ones with difficult working conditions, managers also have to submit to the Walmart treatment. Managers talk about their training program as more "indoctrination" than training. A large aspect of their training is how to spot trouble employees, people that might have ideas of bringing in unions or may rebel against the store's employee practices. Store managers receive a bonus if salaries are below a certain threshold. This pressures salaried managers (who don't receive overtime pay) to work more hours without compensation.

And forget having a corner office. Walmart prides itself on keeping management costs low. This means office space, computers and supplies are all tightly managed. No expensive company cars, fancy computers or tablets, or expensive trips to the Caribbean for "management retreats." Managers show the same level of thrift as everywhere else in the organization.

But is Walmart shy about this? Not at all. In fact, they are proud of it. Their entire culture is to keep prices low. And this translates to everything they do, from the management of suppliers and employees, to store conditions. Everything is about efficiency and cost management.

This is their strength. Walmart embraces its personality as an Accountant. And they hire people that fit this mold.

Why is it called it an Accountant?

Most modern accountants are experts at managing finances. Mixing strategic planning skills, analytical insights and real-world pragmatism allows them to optimize the finances of their company. But these aren't the type of accountants we are talking about here.

Our definition of Accountant relies on the stereotypical, cost-focused version of the Accountant. The one that spends hours poring through columns of numbers to find areas to cut, items to reduce or remove. They would gladly buy single-ply, sand paper-like toilet paper for your company's restroom in order to cut a few dollars. They replace the company coffee with a coin-operated, stale coffee machine.

This is our version of the Accountant, which we will distinguish with a capital A. So if you are an accountant by trade, I'm sorry if I've offended you with this title, but I'm sure you will agree it is befitting. And if you are the kind of accountant who does such things as described, then I am not sorry at all.

The Accountant: A definition

Accountants believe ISPs are a necessary evil, something that is essential but that needs to be managed tightly. They worry that users might abuse or steal company resources if left on their own. They believe that controlling users is essential to controlling costs.

Their low-cost orientation makes them care little about users. Not that service is not important to them, but they believe service should be optimized to reduce costs, not help users. For example, Accountants will set service hours from 9 to 5, even when the company is operating 24/7. Do you need service outside of these working hours? Wait till tomorrow.

The low cost orientation also reduces their involvement in business planning and operations. Accountants are seldom found on executive committees or taking part in any type of strategic planning activities. They typically have a courteous but distant relationship with the company's business units.

Traits
Advantages: The Accountant's top 5 competitive advantages

- Careful: Cautious in actions and decisions. Will not take any unnecessary risks and will prefer proven solutions.
- Conscientious: Driven to do what is right for the company. Decisions are guided by what's best at the moment.
- Hard-working: Works with energy and commitment. Doesn't count hours and is fully engaged at all times.
- Practical: Concerned with the actual use of something rather than with theory and ideas. Less concerned with grand ideas and more with day-to-day execution.
- Rational: Acts with reason and logic. Doesn't fall prey to trends, sales pitches or what others are doing.

Pitfalls: Potential areas of weaknesses

- Conservative: Holds on to attitude and beliefs. Doesn't adapt well to new methods, ways of thinking or orientations.

- Inflexible: Unwilling to change or compromise. Doesn't react well to change, preferring the status-quo.

Solutions – Use the old reliable

When my wife was pregnant with our daughter, we had an obstetrician that had been practicing for more than 30 years. My wife was asking which kind of medication she could take while pregnant and he kept saying "Use the old reliable, aspirin and such." His point was to use medication that had been on the market for years since all possible side effects would have been uncovered and understood by now. It was the easiest way to reduce risk for the baby.

The Accountants use the same metaphor for the solutions they delivers to clients. Whether they're deploying a new compensation plan, a software solution or legal advice, the Accountant will typically "Use the old reliable." Whenever a new trend in the industry appears, the Accountant will wait for others to test it and break their noses on it before using it. Even then, the solution better provide some really great benefits for the Accountant to jump aboard.

I had a client who was proud that he had been running the same financial application for twenty years. And he would have kept using it for another twenty if the provider hadn't gone out of business. For the Accountant, old is a benefit.

Service - We'll be there between 8:00 and 17:00

If you've moved recently you understand how painful it can be to get your house setup with services. Whether it is cable, phone or gas, most providers give you a very large window of the time they will show up for installation. And you better be there when they show up, or else you will be rescheduled two weeks later.

Accountants build their services based on what works best for them, not on what's best for clients. It isn't rare to see Accountants provide service only during regular business hours while the rest of the company operates 24/7. Accountants build their service so that it reduces costs and makes things simpler for them. Having multiple service shifts would cost more in overtime and make management more complex. After all, how will the Accountant know if people that work nights are actually working?

The Accountant will get to your request when it is convenient. It's not that they deliver bad service. But they prioritize their work based on what they feel is most urgent. And they don't necessarily bother informing you on the status of your request, which can leave users frustrated, not knowing when it will be handled, or if it will be handled at all.

People - Working hard to keep the status quo

Accountant leaders are very hands on, to the point where they make most of the decisions for their department. They are aware of every activity that is happening in the department, and provide guidance and direction for most of them. In fact, their leadership style is so geared toward control that most of their staff defer any decision to them. The Accountant will typically sign all contracts, authorize all expenses and meet with providers.

Staff typically are very loyal to the company they work for. It is common to see people work all their lives for the same company. Despite this level of loyalty, staff typically knows very little about the company they work for. They are not encouraged to spend time with their business counterparts, simply because they don't believe it serves a purpose. This leaves very few opportunities for the staff of the Accountant to make any decisions.

Accountants are typically centralized, preferring to keep all of their people in one location where it is easier to control their work.

Governance - How much will this cost?

Would you spend a penny to gain quarter? Most people would say yes, but not necessarily Accountants. Especially if the penny came from their budget and the quarter went to someone else's.

Every single initiative typically starts with the Accountants asking "How much will this cost". Then they ask about returns, risk, etc. But the very first preoccupation of the Accountant is to keep a balanced budget and keep costs as low as possible. And for a very good reason. The Accountant knows that every initiative ends up costing more than planned, and can have a negative impact on their operational budget for years afterwards.

Accountants typically have very little need for complex governance structure. Why? Because Accountants don't start many projects to begin with. And when new projects do get started, it's typically because the company no longer has a choice. The Accountant will begin new initiatives if a new regulation has taken effect, if a product is no longer supported or if the boss explicitly asks for it. And the Accountants prefer to start new projects only when they come from the boss. This way, they know that the request is a priority for the company and they accept it will have consequences on budgets.

Budgets - A penny saved is a penny earned

Accountants are masters at keeping their budget stable. They work tirelessly to reduce expenses to offset the increasing cost of living. They consistently rate well when they benchmark their operations against peers.

They are masters at optimizing costs. They will pore over contracts, making sure that the supplier delivered everything as promised, and if not they will cut their payment. They manage overtime very aggressively, encouraging people to "bank" their days instead. They will review cell phone usage and frequently question the staff about the high number of minutes they use. They know their budget inside out, and are able to quote the exact cost of almost all the services they use.

The Accountants are also great at managing surprises. They will typically hide money everywhere in their budget, so that if something unexpected happens they will be able to tackle it without going over budget.

Performance measures - Budget is everything

The Accountants use few performance measures, and for very good reasons: they know exactly what is happening. They are so involved in the day-to-day operations of the business that they know if someone is not productive, if an asset is under performing, or if there are new issues.

The only real measure of performance for the Accountant is the budget.

Where to find the Accountant - Stable and cost conscious

Accountants can typically be found in companies that are stable and run on low margins, for instance manufacturing and transportation. The stability of the company allows the Accountant to evolve slowly, minimizing risks and conserving capital. The culture of these companies typically promotes a tight control over workers and sometimes have difficult labor relations, which fits well with the Accountant's personality.

Strategies for the Accountant

The Accountant is a master at managing its budget and reducing costs. His eagle eye view allows him to see opportunities that no one else saw. But his intense focus on productivity can have dramatic impact on the level of service it provides. To be successful, the Accountant need to focus on service delivery as much as it does on its finances. We've identified three strategies to help the Accountant deliver amazing value.

1. Become predictable

A common source of frustration from users is the unpredictability of the service that Accountants provide. Some days the service is good, other days it may take forever because a new priority came in. This can have disastrous effect on Accountant's reputation, making him seen as an unpredictable and unreliable partner.

The Accountant can raise the level of satisfaction (or at least reduce dissatisfaction) by establishing standards for services. They should focus on setting expectations concerning timing right at the beginning when assigning work "you should complete this by Friday," and reset these expectations if a new priority arises "Sorry, it will take two more days to fill your request, a new priority came in." Having a consistent standard will help clients set their expectations appropriately and will also help the Accountant manage its own service performance.

2. Measure service performance

The Accountant is a master with number. He understands the variations in its budgets and in the productivity of his staff. It is not unusual to see the Accountant pouring over detailed financial tables describing the expenses, challenging variations and setting new performance standards.

But one thing the Accountant typically fails to measure is the performance of its service, *as perceived by the users*. The Accountant internal view often doesn't reflect the reality that users perceive. The Accountant's team might be very efficient and productive, but users might still see long delays and poor service. By taking an external view of its service, the Accountant can measure the perception of his service and identify factors that influence the quality of the service delivered. This often opens the door to service improvement without impacting operational costs. It also helps the accountant manage its reputation by being able to demonstrate the real performance of his team, as opposed to the water cooler rumours.

3. Experiment with new initiatives

The Accountant's competitive advantage is to remain skeptical, while everyone else is trying the latest ideas and solutions. This leaves the Accountant behind the curve in term of adoption, but also in term of experimentation and learning. It also contributes to the Accountant's reputation of conservatism and risk-avoidance by the other members of the executive team.

The Accountant should invest a small portion of their resources toward new initiatives that offer a good potential for return. Trying new technologies, business practices or approaches will familiarize the staff with them and make adoption easier in the future. This will also show the rest of the organization that Accountants are not as rigid as everyone might be thinking.

Misconceptions
The Accountant delivers terrible service

Focusing on cutting costs doesn't necessarily have to mean delivering bad service. At Walmart, for example (the ultimate Accountant), the service isn't bad. The service isn't great either, but no one comes out of Walmart saying that the cashier was rude, that there was only one register open and customers had to wait for hours.

Actually, providing bad service goes against the Accountant's ultimate goal, which is to reduce costs.

The Accountant realizes that if people stop calling for support, problems will escalate and correcting issues will become very complicated. In fact, Accountants would rather that users not try to fix problems on their own, and should instead call right away when a problem occurs. Most go so far as locking computers, so users can't access administrative functions.

The excuse of delivering bad service because they are Accountants simply doesn't work.

The Accountant doesn't care about its users

The Accountant wants its users to be productive. Being an Accountant is a difficult and unrewarding job. Their service is clearly seen as a cost centre, something that we would rather be able to do without, but are stuck with. So we might as well optimize it, so it costs as little as possible.

Working for the Accountant

Working for an Accountant can be challenging. Their management style can make it difficult to introduce new ideas and methods, preferring time-tested methods. The Accountants are also very careful about trusting employees, leaving very little margin for error and decision-making discretion. One way to gain the trust of an Accountant is to show that you are in control of your budget.

1. Know your costs cold

My department was reviewing the company's contract for teleconference services, something we used quite a bit since we were distributed across 22 sites. To me it was an easy project, simply select the right supplier and transition to it, so I gave it to one of the junior project managers to use as a learning exercise. A few days after the contract was signed, I got a call from my chairman late at night, an Accountant, asking me how much the new supplier costs were compared to the previous supplier. I replied casually that the new costs were 0.06$ per minute, compared to 0.08$ per minute in the past. He replied was that he could have sworn they were more like 0.07$ a minute in the past.

Having some doubts, I emailed the project manager asking for the actual costs. Turns out the chairman was right, it was 0.07$ in the past. And then the magnitude of the situation hit me: the chairman of a billion dollar company knew, by heart, the telecom costs that were less than 20,000$ per year, while I didn't remember something we did a few days ago.

The Accountants expect you to know your budget inside out, because most likely they know your budget very well. You should understand all of the factors that have an impact on your budget such as suppliers' costs, HR, supplies, etc. The Accountants will routinely question you about factors that drive your costs, and chances are they already know the answer. Faking answers, hoping to gain some time, will only result in losing your credibility.

2. Be proactive about optimizing costs

Accountants often use an interesting technique to reduce costs. They will pick a number at random (typically 10%) and cut the budget by that much, asking people to make it happen. No grand analysis, no comparisons, nothing. Simply a random number that is achievable. And in response, people typically find sufficient savings to be able to meet the target. Thus, a simple fishing expedition comes back positive for the Accountant. And the basis for this is that the Accountants believe that there are always opportunities for optimization, and people simply need to be sufficiently motivated to make it happen.

Don't wait to be challenged. Most often, the Accountant simply wants to be reassured that you are managing costs tightly, and nothing shows this better than regularly finding opportunities. Whether it's 10% or not, the simple act of questioning expenses and cutting them when necessary shows you are proactive about managing your budget.

3. Manage risks

Accountants are often coerced into doing projects simply because they don't have a choice. Say a software package is no longer supported and must be upgraded, a new regulation forces a retrofit on half the fleet, or the CEO got talked into doing an employee engagement project by a HR firm.

The Accountant hates surprises. Understanding future costs and managing to avoid / minimize them not only keep costs low now, but shows that you are ready to face any surprises in the future.

In our next chapter, we'll look at the Butler, the most user-friendly of all ISP personalities. The Butler and Accountant are often at odds, fighting about the fine line between not wanting to accommodate users and not being able to (due to lack of funds, for example).

Can you remember times when you experience great service? Perhaps at a restaurant or a hotel? Chances are you were served by a Butler, someone who lives to serve.

The Butler

Great tasting coffee, at 4$ a cup

Starbucks achieved something that other companies dream of: they turned a commodity product (coffee) into a premium experience. No one would have thought it possible for a company to charge more than 4$ for a cup of coffee, and have people lined up to buy it. Especially with Dunkin Donuts, Tim Horton's and McDonald selling it for around a dollar. And Starbucks achieved this not by selling coffee made from premium beans (in taste tests Starbucks often rates lower than McDonald's) but by selling an experience.

Starbucks has defined their entire company around great customer service. In the morning you are served quickly and efficiently, and then you can come back in the afternoon to sit and work at a table in a nice casual atmosphere, and in the evening go on a date with your spouse in a nice chilled-out ambiance. All in the same establishment.

Starbucks achieves this through a relentless focus on employee development. Each Starbucks employee goes through intensive training that includes the basics of coffee, customer service excellence, managing their emotions, and dealing with difficult situations.

Starbucks' managers spend a lot of their time reviewing employee performance and they emphasize customer satisfaction on a daily basis. They continually provide positive reinforcement and feedback.

Starbucks' service is reactive. They are there when you need them.

They spend all their time preparing so that when you do show up, the entire experience is as good as you can expect.

Why being a Butler works for Starbucks

Starbucks delivers superior service, and their customers are willing to pay a premium for it. The atmosphere, service and brand are as much part of the product as the coffee itself.

How does this apply to internal service providers?

First, being a Butler is not about saying yes to everything. Starbucks doesn't offer donuts or five course meals. They have a menu and stick to it. They offer a fairly limited set of services that they deliver very well.

Secondly, service is the core of Starbuck's offering. They adapt their service depending on the situation (quick service in the morning, personalized service after rush hour). Butlers tend to do the same thing. They adapt their service levels based on the time of year, for example the end of year crunch.

Butlers provide service through people. For sure they have the tools and processes they need, but they realize that it's the people that make the difference. This is why they focus much of their time on training and actively manage employees on a daily basis. Butlers typically spend time listening to support calls and giving guidance on how the call could have gone better.

Why call it a Butler?

Alfred is probably the most well-known butler in history. If you are not familiar with Alfred, he is Batman's butler. And most importantly, he manages Batman's covert identity, allowing him to fight crime without having to worry about what's happening back home.

But Alfred also does things he'd rather not do. When Batman is injured and should not be going to fight crime, Alfred still helps him suit up and send him on his way. But yet, he never tries to influence "Master Wayne." Instead he is always there for him, anticipating his every need and request.

This is what differentiates Butlers from the other personality profiles. They are always there for their clients and they will go to great lengths to fulfill their needs. And they will do this even if they don't agree with these needs.

Who is the Butler?

The Butlers have a strong desire to satisfy their users. They realize that their organization depends on them and are more than willing to be a strong support player. They believe that every user should be treated like a paying customer and should not only be satisfied but should also be able to fully depend on them.

Butlers thrive in areas where users are very knowledgeable and demanding with respect to ISPs.

Traits
Advantages: The Butler's top 5 competitive advantages
- Compassionate: Feels sympathy and concerns for others. Understands the situation of others and offers support.
- Courteous: Polite and respectful in their manners. Always treats users and colleagues with the outmost respect.
- Friendly: Kind and pleasant. Works to maintain a kind, pleasant atmosphere and avoid conflict.
- Helpful: Always ready to help out. Will stop everything at the drop of a hat to help a user or colleague in need.
- Versatile: Able to adapt to different situations. Will easily accommodate the requirements of their users or partners and change their work methods accordingly.

Pitfalls: Potential areas of weaknesses
- Inconsistent: Service delivery is not always uniform. The

crisis of the day often takes priority over everything else.
- Indecisive: Has difficulties making tough decisions, especially if it impacts users negatively. Butlers often overcommit due to their inability to say no.

Where we can find the Butler

The Butler is often found in industries where knowledge workers abound. These workers are typically sophisticated, understand their needs very precisely and keep up to date with the trends in their industry. Users often know better than anyone else what their needs are, and only need someone to deliver the service to them.

Examples of such industries are engineering, design, law, consulting, research and development and media. The needs of these users are often very specialized and vary across the company, which makes it difficult for an ISP to be knowledgeable in as many areas as the users.

Solution - Ice cream and pickles? No problems.

Luxury hotels are fantastic when it comes to serving guests. They understand that when people are away from home (especially business people) and spending from their company's expense account, they can be very demanding. And weird. For example, one guest asked for 100 plastic flamingos to be placed in one of his friend's room, probably as a practical joke (the concierge only guessed, as he never asked why). Another asked for a nuptial room for the first night of Black Magic and Cricket as bride and groom, two dogs that got married earlier in the day. The Hotel was happy to leave them welcome gifts of squeaky bones.

Just like concierges, Butlers don't judge, they deliver. They're focused on delivering a high level of customer service and try to respond to every user need.

The solutions Butlers provide are those that users ask for. But contrary to hotels, Butlers are not proactive in their search for solutions. While perfectly happy to respond to the requests of users, they will not be looking ahead and proposing solutions by themselves. Butlers lack the business knowledge (low business orientation) to be able to offer meaningful solutions to users' needs. They don't follow the industry of their internal clients and are typically not aware of what others are doing. This often leads to sub-optimal solutions or duplication across the organization.

You've probably seen companies with two or three customer relationship management (CRM) solutions, since the sales team and the marketing team couldn't agree on one single solution. Or an IT department that supported only PCs, except for one department that absolutely wanted to have Apple computers. The Butler is only happy to accommodate these requests even if it proves to increase costs in the long term and even create issues (like having customer information spread across different databases).

Service - How can I help you?
The Butler is always ready to serve. The Butlers sets service level commitments (a description of the services they provide and the performance standards for each). But these are only indicative, as they typically like to exceed these standards. The Butlers promise new hires to be done in two weeks? They'll try to have it done in one week. Month-end close in five days? Let's do it in three. The Butlers don't believe in under-promising and over-delivering, but instead promise a lot and deliver even more.

The Butlers also thrive in responding to complex, demanding requests. While they try to streamline their services, they also don't mind adapting to the different needs of internal clients.

For example, I once worked with an accounts payable team that had different processes depending on the supplier. The procurement team had special relationships with key suppliers and wanted to keep them happy. So they asked payables for all sorts of unconventional business practices, such as sending a check by courier the very same day the invoice came in, or even paying the supplier when the order was made (even if the material hadn't been delivered yet). And the payables team was happy to oblige, even if it required extra labour to handle all of these exceptions.

The service is also closely aligned with the needs of the business. The Butler will follow the hours of operations of the business, creating different shifts if necessary, or having people "on call", always available to respond to user requests day and night. It is not unusual for Butlers to check their emails on their days off to see if any requests came in so they can respond to them immediately.

People - Stressed-out but willing

We often refer to someone who likes to solve crises as a firefighter. After all, the most important work a firefighter does is to spend their days waiting for a fire, and then jumping in their trucks and working tirelessly to put it out. They frequently work 24 hours straight to put out fires and save lives. But when you talk with a firefighter he will tell you a different story. For them, the most important work they do is going house to house making sure that fire alarms and extinguishers are in place, that the fireplaces are swept and that new construction is built to code. Their most important work is to prevent fires from happening in the first place.

Butlers are stereotypical firefighters, driven by crisis. They jump on every opportunity to resolve an issue or solve a problem. Very talented at managing situations, they keep their cool and remain completely focused on the task at hand. Multiple fires at the same time? No problem, they'll prioritize and assign resources to contain the situation and make sure that no fires are left unattended.

But unlike firefighters, the Butler isn't as good at making sure fires don't happen in the first place. Butlers are so focused on meeting client's demands and managing crises that they often neglect more mundane activities such as general management, planning and risk management. It wouldn't be unusual for a Butler to use the only fire extinguisher and then be stuck without one when a new fire occurs. As much as they would like to take the time to plan and be proactive, there is always a crisis that pulls Butlers away from these activities. This leaves the department in a continual reactive mode.

The staff of Butlers are also focused on managing crisis. In fact, it quickly becomes the only management style they know. Most Butlers complain that they've lost control over their days and have a hard time prioritizing work, letting the day's event dictate their schedule. One even went so far as telling me, "I love my work, every day I don't know what I'll be doing!"

This constant focus on the crisis of the day often leaves employees stressed-out and having a higher than normal rate of burn-out. The Butler's inability to say no forces the team to be creative to meet all requests, and when creativity fails it is replaced by simply working more hours. It's not unusual to see employees working nights and week-ends to move requests or projects forward.

Governance - When do you need it?

There is an old cliché saying that construction workers always deliver their work late. If you've ever contracted a house to be built, then you will probably say it isn't a cliché at all. The reality is that competition is fierce in the construction sector, and if an entrepreneur tells a client he doesn't have the time to take on his work, then he will probably lose the contract to someone else. So they often end up taking in more than they can handle, leaving them to work long days while still delivering their work late.

Butlers have a similar attitude. They've never seen a project they didn't like. The Butler's governance process tends to be fairly simple: "If the users asked for it, then it must be important." Butlers typically don't challenge the requests from their clients, relying on them to only ask for things that are truly essential. When new requests come in they simply add them to the list of on-going work. Of course this list often becomes extremely long, to the point of becoming unrealistic.

Butlers let crises dictate the priorities. A new regulation came in and we must comply before December 31st? Let's tackle it first. A vice-president is starting to complain that his project is not moving forward? Let's focus on that. Prioritization is often done based on decibels; whoever yells the highest.

The Butler's conflict aversion leads them to delay communicating bad news, trying instead to fix the situation by either working harder or simply refusing to acknowledge there is an issue. Of course, this can become extremely frustrating for their clients.

Budget - How much were you looking to spend?
Butlers have a tough time managing a budget. Not because they are not financially astute, far from it. But since they don't like to say no, it causes situations where they spend their budget to the limit. And when issues arise, the budget is exceeded regularly.

Successful Butlers realize this issue and in response prefer to let the clients manage the budgets. For example, Butlers typically have a small operational budget appropriate to their needs, but no funds for project initiatives. When internal clients ask for projects, they will "subsidize" the Butler by transferring budgets. Sometimes Butlers will go as far as charging for the use of its services (chargeback) to make sure that the budget is really aligned with the needs of its users. The philosophy being "if they are willing to pay for it then it must be what they need."

Butlers don't like to benchmark themselves to their peers since they know the results will be unfavourable. Butlers customize their service to each user and therefore cannot maintain the same level of operational efficiency as others.

Performance measures: All about the users

Butlers measure their success based on what the users think. Most of their metrics revolve around service performance and satisfaction.

Typical metrics would include:
- Service response time (how quickly they took charge of a problem)
- Service resolution time (how quickly they resolved a problem)
- User satisfaction (based on satisfaction surveys)

The Butlers are very diligent about monitoring metrics and making sure they stay within performance standards. But Butlers seldom communicate these metrics, not wanting to appear boastful.

Strategies

The Butler already knows how to deliver amazing service. His constant preoccupation with the welfare of its users give him a natural advantage when it comes time to satisfy its clients. But the Butler's pitfalls can also relegate him to a commodity provider. The Butler tends to be invisible, and its value is also taken for granted. We've identified three strategies to help the Butler build its strengths and avoid its common pitfalls.

1. Plan initiative for the next three years

Butlers are typically not inclined to plan work ahead of time, which leads to taking in more than they can handle. To counteract this tendency to overextend themselves, the Butlers should develop a plan of all the initiatives they will tackle in the next three years. Chances are there is already enough work identified to completely fill the capacity for the next few years anyway.

This list then becomes the tool to manage governance. Every time a new project or initiative is identified, something else from the list must be removed or resources added. The Butlers don't have to make this call, they can leave the company to do its own prioritization.

2. Respect your service level commitment

Butlers can manage their client's expectations by being consistent in their service delivery. Instead of trying to deliver faster than promised, they can simply deliver exactly as planned. Sounds counter-intuitive? Clients set their expectations based on their previous experience. If the Butler consistently beats its estimates, the clients will expect the Butler to beat its estimates every single time. Clients will be dissatisfied when the Butler simply delivers on time.

Respecting commitments sometimes means waiting to deliver the work to a client, even if it is completed, something that is very difficult for a Butler. Why wait, we have an opportunity to delight the client?

3. Measure and report on exceptions

Butlers love to handle crises, and frankly they are quite good at it. But a business cannot be managed in crisis-mode all the time. The constant adrenaline rush to get the job done not only becomes very taxing on the individuals involved, it also push asides less urgent but important work that needs to be done (such as planning for example).

Since they have a hard time saying no, the Butlers can educate the business instead on the quantity and impact of the crisis. By measuring and reporting on the number of crisis the Butler handled during the course of a given month, it can demonstrate that perhaps not everything is as critical as clients make them to be. Is it normal that 35% of requests are considered crisis? Are they really crisis? This also allows the Butler to demonstrate the consequences of handling crisis such as projects being delayed for example.

Working for the Butler

Working for a Butler requires a constant understanding of what is happening. The Butler's preoccupation with customer service forces everyone to be fully aware of every issues that are on the radar. The Butler also like to jump in when crisis happens, which can be difficult to manage when there are more chefs than cooks in the kitchen. One way to earn the trust of the Butler is to be always thinking of the impact any decisions will have on the users. The three strategies below will help you to earn the Butler's trust.

1. Know your customers

The Butlers know everyone that's worth knowing in your company. Not only do they know them by name, but chances are they know quite a bit about each of them, including how they get along with each other. The head of finance hates the head of IT? Butlers know that already.

By understanding the different players and the relative power they hold, it makes it easier for the Butler to manage crisis and make sure it maintains a good reputation for its department. And by developing personal relationship with these key players, the Butler can be reassured that you are delivering the best possible service to meet their needs.

2. Know the status of the crisis of the day

If you work for a Butler and have staff reporting to you, you're in for a frustrating experience. Butlers like to be kept up to date in real-time of the status of any issues happening. They want fresh news all the time and typically avoid layers to get it, going straight to the source. This means you should expect your boss to frequently by-pass you and get updates from your staff directly.

By always being in the loop you can position yourself as the go-to person for fresh updates. The Butler will be reassured that you are indeed managing (or at least staying close) the crisis and will typically move on to another one.

3. Know your service performance

Butlers invite users to complain directly to them. And when they do get a complaint, they react aggressively to discover what happened and fix it. This means you may be getting regular phone calls asking why Bob in marketing didn't get his computer yet or why it is taking so long to fill the position in sales.

By understanding your service performance (and its variation) you should already know if one or more service levels haven't been reached and be able to give a status update on the fly. This proactive view of service performance prevents surprises. The Butler hates hearing bad news directly from the clients. The more advanced notice you can give him, the easier it will be to manage the perceptions.

4. Complement your boss: Plan your work

One of the major problems with Butlers is their lack of forward planning. Butlers are so caught up in the day-to-day operational aspect of their ISP that they tend to have little time to sit back and plan ahead.

You can help by understanding your own capacity and prioritizing work. By developing a long-term action plan you can identify potential issues ahead of time (such as resources constraints or conflicts between projects) and help the Butler avoid problems while they still can.

The other side of the coin

At the other end of the spectrum is the Nanny. Nannies are almost the exact opposite of the Butler. While the Butler lives to serve, Nannies have an agenda of their own and the users are only a piece of it.

Are you the kind of person that doesn't like making decisions, that prefers to follow a path already traced? Chances are you would get along with a Nanny, who loves telling others what to do.

The Nanny

Apple the Nanny

Apple (the company) is a perfect Nanny. It knows what users need better than the users do.

Walk with me through the experience of buying an Apple product. First you enter the store (or buy online). Your choices are limited: do you want a computer that sits on a desk or one that you can take with you? That's pretty much it. Of course there are variations (for power users, for example) but their product line is severely limited. But rest assured that with a Mac you can grab any box and it will work when you get home.

Then you open the box. The computer asks which language you prefer, your network and where you live. Then it starts up, just like that. No long configurations or the inclusion of dozens of trial software items that fill up your desktop and want you to upgrade and register.

Apple builds its products for simplicity. You could also say that it assumes its users are dumb. Either way, they work.

Apple is famous for not doing market research. How could they? Since they reinvent categories regularly, market research data would probably be irrelevant.

Apple decides what's good for you. While most companies work hard to make the transition smooth for their customers, Apple has no shame in reinventing everything. Still have software on CDs? Sorry, you should have thought of that before buying a MacBook Air since it doesn't come with a dvd drive.

This changes everything. Again.

Apple has been the dominant driver in the tech sector for more than ten years now, crushing competitors with their music players, phones, tablets and computers. They've taken what were once generic "beige" components and turned them into objects of desire for technical and non-technical people.

Apple is not known for their great customer service either. Yes, they have great looking stores, cool salespeople, and "geniuses" to help with your computer problems, but getting access to the geniuses can be time consuming. They are not known for their easy replacement policy either. If there is a problem, you may have to live without your computer for days before it is fixed.

They also are not open with their roadmaps. You never know what the next iPhone will look like, or how the next iMac will perform. The $2000 you just spent on a MacBook might very well be worthless in six months when a new model changes everything, again.

Apple seems to know what people want before they want it. They've focused much of their differentiation on design, making their products not only very different in appearance, but also stretching the limits of materials and components to make devices that are lighter, smaller and, of course, more expensive.

They also put a lot of energy into making things simple for their users. Most of their equipment and software is fairly intuitive, and easy to learn and use. Their applications tend to mimic real-word objects and contain only the minimum of buttons and components.

Apple designs shine by what's missing, just as much as by what's there.

Apple's innate understanding of what people want in a tech device (ease of use, status, etc.) has allowed them to create entirely new demand for entirely new products, and dominate their market.

Why being a Nanny works for Apple
Apple's sole differentiation is through design. They create little works of art that people want to own, use and be seen with. Their products are status symbols. Their focus on good design allows them to meet customer demands, and create new demands.

How does this apply to internal service providers?
Apple knows a lot more about design than we do. Nannies tend to also know a lot more about the business than their users. Understanding what drives the business and how it will evolve allows the Nanny to be one step ahead of everyone.

However, Apple is very selective in its design. They provide few options and fewer components. Nannies tend to limit user choices by providing them what they need and only what they need. They won't offer duplicate solutions if they can avoid it.

Finally, Apple keeps things very simple. Nannies tend to remove all the functionalities and components that are not required by a user. This makes applications and systems much easier to learn, and also reduces support calls by limiting possible causes of problems.

Why call it a Nanny
Ever see the reality-TV show Supernanny? Every week the Supernanny (Fran) visits families where the kids are real brats. Not the run of the mill brat, but real horrors that yell, bite and throw objects at their parents. And through her unique set of British discipline, structure and patience she transforms the kids into well-

behaved children. Of course, throughout the show we see that it was never the kids fault at all but instead the failures of their parents that made them into monsters.

What's interesting about the Supernanny is that she offers a service, but as she does she takes control of the family. Rules are established that children and parents need to follow. In a nutshell, she knows what's best for everyone.

Our Nannies are similar. They deliver services to help end-users, but their focus is not on serving them well or meeting their every need, but rather to keep them productive. And if to do so they have to make rules, order time-outs and make lists of chores, so be it.

The Nanny: A definition

The Nanny is the driving force behind the adoption of processes within their organization. Their unique understanding of the business as well as subject-matter allows them to know what the organization and its users need to become more productive.

Just like a real nanny, they guide users in the right direction, ensuring they learn, are productive, and obey the rules.

Their relentless focus on improving business processes often results in higher costs, but those costs are always justified with a great return on investments.

Traits

Advantages: The Nanny's top 5 competitive advantages

- Decisive: Has the ability to make decisions quickly and effectively. Doesn't second guess and would rather make the wrong choice than do nothing.
- Determined: Once a decision is made, resolved not to change it. Will not let doubt or uncertainty change the course of action.

- Forceful: Strong and assertive. Imposes views and actions on others.
- Independent: Doesn't depend on others.
- Self-disciplined: Control their own conduct. Maintain rigorous work standards and practices.

Pitfalls: Potential areas of weaknesses
- Detached: Not closely associated with the company. Don't really see themselves as part of the team.
- Ruthless: Doesn't have compassion for others. Will drive initiatives forward regardless of the consequences for others.

Where the Nanny can be found
The Nanny can frequently be found in the retail sector. With employee turnover rates as high as 40%, retail organizations have a hard time managing this constant inflow of people. Fortunately, the Nannies are very good at putting together processes and controlling the work done by the users. Public service is also an important breeding ground for Nannies where they can develop and monitor processes to control the vast masses of public sector employees.

Nannies can also be found in any type of company that is going through a profound change or business transformation. In these situations Nannies are often more of a mercenary, being selected for a specific mandate of a few years and then moving on. This allows the company to implement drastic change and let all the employee resentment leave with the Nanny's departure.

Solution - It's not because you are essential that you are important
Henry Ford revolutionized the manufacturing world with the invention of the assembly line. Instead of having the workers go back and forth while the vehicle stayed at one pace, he realized he could gain significant productivity advantages by having the vehicles move in front of the worker's station. And the workers could specialize and

become even more productive by doing the same work over and over again. Of course, assembly line work is debilitating for the workers, but the cars are great.

Nannies have an exact vision of how they want to see the organization in the future. And more dangerously, they have a plan to get there. Their high business orientation gives them great insight into how the business operates and can easily see the opportunities for improvement. They also understand the competitive landscape and know what it takes to overtake competitors.

Nannies loves predictability and a lot of their solutions revolve around either controlling how employees work or removing them altogether. The nanny will often focus on initiatives that will automate parts of the organization, reducing the company's dependency on human capital. Nannies will develop procedures and systems to control how employees work, interact with their customers and optimize their productivity.

Of course, the Nannies are open to user recommendations. And in some cases, they might even implement a few of them. But only if it doesn't contradict initiatives or standards that are already in place. Nannies will often be systematic about it, allocating a specific portion of their budget for user requests, or as the saying goes, "buying the peace."

Service - Users as cattle

When I worked for an animal recycling company I was treated to some interesting experiences, one of which was to visit a slaughterhouse for pigs. One thing that really struck me was how the plant director insisted that the pigs had to wait three hours after they arrived before they could be slaughtered. His reasoning was that it gave time for the pigs to relax after the long trip by truck. I was a bit surprised by this, especially considering the nature of the work was to kill animals. Of course, this wasn't for the animals per se, the reasoning was that a stressed out animal doesn't taste as good, and three hours is the minimum amount of time to let the animal flush out all of the stress hormones. Compassionate, stress-free bacon.

A humorist once said "I love my public... as a group. I don't want to see any individuals showing up at my door at night". Contrary to what we can believe, Agents love their users. After all, Agents are in a support role and their primary responsibility is to empower them so they can get their job done. But the Agents love their users the same way a farmer loves his cattle: as a group.

Retailers face an extremely high level of employee turnover (as high as 40% for some). This means that the HR department is extremely busy with recruiting, but it also has to be extremely efficient in training those employees so they can be productive during their very short employment. A retailer client of mine was facing a situation with employee engagement and wondering what HR could do to make things better. My first reaction was to ask if they considered doing an employee engagement survey to identify the pain points, something fairly common in retail organizations. His first reaction was to tell me, "Well, I don't really care what they think, I only want them to be working hard." I could sense he immediately regretted this outburst, but it was the attitude of HR at this company. They had training programs and on boarding practices that were designed to make the employees as productive as possible as quickly as possible. This is in the same way that a cattle farmer will give antibiotics to its pigs not to keep the animals healthy, but to reduce losses.

This approach to user management works well for some industries like retail. But this attitude can conflict with the users who resent being "managed" so openly, especially knowledge workers, who are in an industry where the employees are very aware that they are the lifeblood of the company.

People - Have gun, will travel

Ernest Shackleton, a famous adventurer who tried to cross the Antarctic continent in 1914 ran the most interesting help wanted ad:

"Men wanted for hazardous journey. Low wages, bitter cold, long hours of complete darkness. Safe return doubtful. Honour and recognition in event of success."

Who would have answered this ad? No one in their right mind, that's for sure. We'll I'd bet that most of the people that did apply were Nannies. Nannies are always up for a challenge. They are always looking to measure themselves against something difficult, for fame and glory but mostly for personal satisfaction.

The Nanny is a strong leader. Decisive, they don't shy away from making decisions. This comes easily for Nannies since they possess a very strong vision of how things should be. Decision-making is thus simply a matter of selecting the option that fits best with their vision. Once the decision is made they also don't second guess their decisions, preferring to let it run its course even if it is wrong. Not because they believe that they don't make mistakes, but because they realize that inaction is worse than taking the wrong road. This attitude can be perceived as being arrogant when really it is just an attempt to keep the momentum going.

Nannies are also very focused. Once they set a target, they will do everything they can to achieve it. And by everything, they really mean everything. They will go to great lengths to keep commitments. Very creative, they will find ways around obstacles that no one would have considered and will use every shortcut in the book to make things happen. This will often upset the purist who would prefer to have things done well rather than quickly. But Nannies would rather have something ok today than something better tomorrow.

The people working for the Nanny tend to also be very smart and focused. The Nanny hires the best and will often use outside help when needed (consultants, contractors, etc.). Teams rely on the Nanny to set the direction and may feel lost when the Nanny is not there to guide things forward. It takes a while for the team to earn the Nanny's trust, but once they do they will be provided with autonomy and latitude, as long as they keep delivering. Sharp, intelligent people typically love working for Nannies as they allow them to experiment with new approaches and take risks.

Governance - Rules are for other people

A few years ago iPads were all the rage. They were just coming out and everyone wanted one. Of course, users had very good business reasons to want one: "My productivity will soar!", "I will be able to work right in front of the client!" Of course, IT departments saw right through this and most decided to wait before deploying iPads to see how effective they really could be. Most IT departments used claims of "security" and "standards compatibility" to justify their decision.

But a funny thing started happened. Some IT workers started using iPads. They would show up at meetings with one of the coveted tablets. Of course, this caused quite a turmoil, with users wondering, "How come people in IT get iPads but we can't?" And IT quickly responded that they were "testing", "experimenting" to see if the iPad could be a viable solution in the future. But the reality was that most of them just wanted an iPad.

That's typical Nanny behaviour. Rules are for others. The ISP has a good mechanism that allows the business to make decisions on future projects? Well, this project is a priority, so there is no need for approval. A corporate standard exists for types of hotels and restaurants when we travel? Well, in this case we have to go to this particular hotel, so we'll skip the rules for now.

Nannies see themselves as above the rules because in most cases, they are the ones making the rules. This is why it is not unusual to see

IT departments with new computers even though the company has a clear standard that we keep them for four years. Or HR accelerates the recruitment of a new HR employee simply because they need them as soon as possible. And finance controls the budgets very tightly and won't let you overspend, but finds hidden pockets of money when their project really needs to get done.

This looseness concerning rules is one of the biggest dissatisfier for Nannies' users. The Nanny's attitude that "Everyone is equal, but we are more equal than others" often leads to frustration and loss of trust. Nothing hurts working relationships more than unfairness and the Nanny is very good at that.

Budget - Let's put everything on black
Would you ever take all your money and bet it on one single project? Chances are you'd want to distribute your resources in several areas to reduce your risk. The Nanny thinks differently. In order to make an impact, Nannies think it is important to narrowly focus their energy and resources, and their budget often reflects that. Nannies aren't shy to invest their entire budget in one major initiative or program, even if it is extremely risky. Nannies will spare no expense to make their initiatives a success, by getting the best resources and making sure they are fully productive.

On the other hand, the Nanny is very cost conscious when it comes to service delivery. The Nanny optimizes costs relentlessly, always trying to reduce operational budgets to the bare minimum. Not as obsessively as the Accountant though. The Accountants reduce costs for the sake of keeping their budgets low, while the Nannies reduce costs in order to free up budget for projects. Every dollar the Nannies put in daily operation is a dollar less they can put in initiatives.

When it comes time to reduce budgets, the Nanny will often prefer to reduce service levels rather than cancel a project. It is not unusual for Nannies to cut service hours, or remove services entirely when budgets are attacked. The Nanny likes to make sure users feel the pain when budgets are reduced, to dissuade further attempts in the future.

Generally though, Nannies tend to have very generous budgets. Their careful planning and operational excellence keeps surprises to a minimum, which allows them to use the emergency funds they like to keep around (just like the Accountant). They are also not shy about "borrowing" resources from other departments, leveraging users or subject matter experts from other groups whenever required.

Performance measures - All about the projects
The Nannies rely on project performance as their prime indicator of success. While they measure operational performance as well, they will often do so just to keep the users in line and prevent them from complaining. But project performance is the name of the game for them and they go to great length to make sure projects are closely monitored and follow efficient but well-defined methodologies.

Strategies
The Nanny is hyper-focused on its objectives. For her, the next three years are fully planned and she know exactly the steps required to get there. She also knows that small, focused teams with aggressive deadlines have much better chances of success than long, drawn-out projects. But the Nanny's can't do everything by herself, she needs to get her team and clients on board with her vision. We've identified three strategies to help the nanny deliver on her visions while reducing the number of potential enemies.

1. Involve users in projects
Nannies hate everything that has the potential to slow down a project. They prefer small teams of highly capable people. This is why Nannies often neglect to involve users in their projects, as they are a potential obstacle to manage. But as we've seen earlier, user involvement is critical for the success of a project.

Successful Nannies develop processes and roles to facilitate the integration of users into their projects. Nannies define guidelines (such as having people work on the project full-time for the duration) to avoid conflict and keep users focused on the task at hand.

2. Follow your own rules

Nannies are really good at developing processes and rules to control the behaviour of their users, but not as good at following the rules themselves. This attitude creates a lot of frustration for the users who sees it as being unfair and elitist.

Nannies should make a conscious effort to obey the same rules as everyone else and not let staff get away with breaking rules either. This means using the same resources as everyone else (no fancy tablet when everyone else can't have one), and following the same processes (starting projects without governance committee approval for example) for decision-making.

3. Communicate more

Nannies have such a clear vision of where they want to go that they often don't see the need to explain themselves in great detail. Either it is too obvious for them, or they get frustrated that others don't keep up. But communicating the vision is a critical piece of getting buy-in and collaboration from the rest of the company.

Nannies should develop a communication plan to communicate their vision, their plan and the resulting impact they will cause on the business. They need to be humble enough to listen to the concerns and adapt their plan whenever possible. By showing empathy for the concerns of others, Nannies will be able to rally people around their vision and make execution so much easier.

Working for a Nanny

Working for a Nanny is a special kind of hell. The Nanny is very focused, to a fault. Nannies will be preoccupied about their on-going projects and the status of their deliverables, at all times. They are very disciplined in their day-to-day activities, and expect the same from their staff. Nannies typically don't tolerate people showing up late or unprepared at meetings. They expect you to plan your work and work the plan. The Nanny will not accept any excuses for a project to be late, and if you are late then you'd better have spent a few all-nighters to show you at least tried. Here are a few strategies to get along with a nanny and complement its pitfalls.

1. Know your projects status

The same way Accountants are obsessed with costs and Butlers with crises, Nannies are obsessed with the status of projects. In the mind of Nannies, each project follow a continuum that represents steps in the execution of their vision. Each project, no matter how trivial, is an important milestone for them. They are also generally obsessed with demonstrating that they are better than everyone else in the business and rarely tolerate mistakes or projects being late.

Of course this implies that you are actively managing your project. Developing a plan, tracking it, and adjusting it when issues arise. It also means that you know the major steps of your project and the associated dates. Chances are the Nanny knows them. You said this phase would be finished by October 31st? Chances are the Nanny will be waiting for you, fully dressed in a Halloween costume, for you to show the completed phase.

Nannies expect you to do miracles to keep your projects on track. This includes being innovative, working like a dog and making people work hard. Nannies won't hesitate to have people come in over a weekend just to meet an artificial deadline. So whatever you commit to, make sure you can actually deliver.

2. Understand the Nanny's vision

Nannies' tremendous focus comes from a crystal clear vision they have for the company. Unfortunately the Nanny isn't a great communicator, so not everyone may be privileged to understand this vision of things to be.

Make sure you do. Ask for clarifications from the Nanny, develop scenarios based on what you know and validate them with the Nanny. Discuss the consequences of different decisions on the future vision. This level of engagement will allow you to gain a better understanding of where the Nanny is going, and also show that you care about the future vision.

3. Stay focused
Don't start initiatives that are not in line with the vision.

For example, a young project manager had a great idea for reducing the costs of the department. By setting up a room to host the servers and migrating some of the servers that were at a supplier's site, they could reduce the monthly co-location cost by almost 5,000$/ month, a saving of 60,000$ per year for an investment of only 30,000$. A pretty good saving. An Accountant would have been thrilled and asked for the project to start right away! But how does the Nanny react? Not very well. The CIO asked the project manager point blank, "Does it look like I need money? Why are you wasting your time on this? Don't you have enough to do?"

Nannies believe that all projects take too long to execute. If you introduce new initiatives, all you are saying is that the current project could be done faster. Instead, focus on the projects underway, the projects that support the Nanny's vision.

4. Complementary: Communicate, become liaison
Nannies biggest struggles are to clearly communicate their vision to the rest of the company. But Nannies have no patience for building relationships with the different stakeholders of the business.

By becoming a liaison between the business and the Nanny you provide a service for both parties. You help the Nanny communicate the message, and make the rest of the business understand how great things will be in the future. In addition, you help the business influence the Nanny's agenda and help them prepare for upcoming changes.

The pseudo-nanny

People often confuse the Nanny with the pseudo-Nanny, an easy mistake since both can be perceived as arrogant and detached. But there is a key difference between the two: real Nannies actually know what they're doing.

The pseudo-Nanny is simply an Accountant with an attitude problem. Accountants have low business orientation, and they know it. They don't try to pretend they know more than anyone else about how to run the business and they don't complain about how the users are incompetent.

On the other hand, pseudo-Nannies believe they are competent and that they know how to run the business, but actually doesn't have the skills or knowledge to do so. They base their opinions on unproved assumptions, relying on comments and their own biased views.

Real Nannies possess a very high level of business knowledge, and understand the industry as well as their own subject matter expertise (IT, HR, Finance, etc.). When Nannies comment on the status of a business process, they are offering not only an opinion but a statement of fact, acquired after a detailed analysis. When a pseudo-Nanny complains about the business, it is often simply the result of complaining and false perceptions.

A Nanny that cares

The Agent is the ISP personality profile with the highest service and business orientation. The Agent's ideal is to achieve perfection. Or is it? The Agent is not happy being left in the corner. In fact, left unchecked, chances are the Agent will lead the organization someday. Perhaps even sooner than expected.

The Agent

Expect Amazing

Weight Watchers is renowned for its weight loss program. They've succeeded at transforming something that can be very complicated into something very easy: counting calories. Most people struggle with weight loss not because of a lack of exercise (although it is a factor) but because they eat too much of the wrong types of food. But counting calories, proteins, carbs and fat in food is very complicated. Weight Watchers has done the work for its members ahead of time and uses a simple point system to make counting calories easy, and planning meals a breeze.

Weight Watchers delivers great customer service. They offer service through a variety of channels and venues (phone, web, group meetings, etc.). They are in-tune with their members' needs and train their front-line employees to deliver excellent and consistent service. Their personnel are often examples of success stories and provide encouragement with a smile.

What makes Weight Watchers a great Agent is in great part their focus on making it simple for their members to follow a diet. Most people have little time and ability to count calories and plan meals. Weight Watchers has devised simple solutions to do so. They understand that overeating is a behavioural problem and so provide support groups, counselling and coaching to help members lose weight.

Weight Watchers use their expertise on losing weight to offer an easy to follow program and resolve issues before they occur. This allows their members to get all the benefits of experts without having to become experts themselves.

Why being an Agent works for Weight Watchers

Weight Watchers is a great Agent because they've made it simple for their members to follow a diet. They provide great service and do not fall into the common trap of making the clients feel bad about their weight problem.

Miracle diets come and go, but none are as easy to apply as the point system of Weight Watchers. And while dieticians would tell you that points are not always consistent, overall Weight Watchers provides a good framework to manage nutrition.

Why call it an Agent?

Have you seen the movie Jerry Maguire? Tom Cruise play a sports agent that leaves a large company with many clients to start his own company, and in the process ends up with only one client, and becomes the best sports agent ever. He follows his client everywhere, advises him, coaches him, and takes care of things so the client can focus on what he does best: play football.

This profile is based on a sports agent for exactly this reason: the Agent allows the users to focus on what they do best. Agents are a real partner to the business because they provide advice, direction and orientation, but they are also responsive to user needs and requests.

It works as long as no one asks "show me the money!"

The Agent: A definition

The Agent believes that ISPs can drive the company to become more competitive and better serve its customers. Agents believe that they need to be actively involved in the majority of the company's business initiatives to have a major and beneficial impact.

Their high service orientation helps them build a strong reputation with their users. They understand that Agents manage business just like an external service provider does and take every issue and request seriously. The Agent also works hard to prevent problems from happening in the first place, investing heavily in proactive maintenance and early diagnostic systems.

The high business orientation gives them a unique perspective on the business. Agents see a clear vision of how the company could run and differentiate itself. They see inefficiencies and interdepartmental problems. But contrary to Nannies, Agents are extremely flexible in their approach. They know how to use every project, initiative and issue in a way to will bring them closer to their vision. Like a master chess player, they see several moves ahead of everyone else, which makes Agents a threat for many executives.

Traits
Advantages: The Agent's top 5 competitive advantages
- Ambitious: Has a strong desire and ambition to succeed. See themselves as the next CEO.
- Communicative: Inclined to share information readily. Always keeps people in the loop on what's happening.
- Creative: Produces original, thought provoking ideas. Finds simple, elegant solutions to almost any problems.
- Diplomatic: Tact and sensitivity in dealing with others. Can rally people around them by addressing their needs / concerns.
- Proactive: Anticipates and controls outcomes. Prevents issues from happening in the first place.

Pitfalls: Potential areas of weaknesses
- Inconsistent: Frequently changes its behaviour, approaches and priorities based on the situation.

- Machiavellian: Unscrupulous in advancing their own career. Won't hesitate to use the political landscape for their own good.

Where we can find the Agent

The Agent can be found in industries that rely heavily on processes, such as financials, banking, insurance or healthcare. Industries that require a high level of innovation are also fertile ground for Agents, including high-tech and information technology.

Agents are also found in more traditional industries where they have successfully built their influence and became an important player in management.

Solution: Global vision, local execution

Chess masters have an amazing ability to anticipate their opponent's moves and evaluate the consequences. It isn't rare for a chess master to analyze 10 or 15 moves ahead of where they currently stand, looking for possible traps and outcomes. Their moves are carefully planned to guide them towards their desired outcome and avoid their opponent's trap.

Agents are similar to the chess grand master as they constantly keep an eye out on the future. They have a good idea of what the future should look like and have a plan to get there. But contrary to the Nanny, Agents are quite flexible in execution. Instead of imposing a very rigid vision and plan to everyone, Agents are much more open and inclusive in planning. In fact, Agents typically don't plan too far in advance, preferring to be flexible in order to accommodate business needs, requests and opportunities.

Every initiative that the Agents tackle is geared toward their vision. And if it doesn't, they'll find a way to transform them. Agents are masters in moving their agenda forward with others or despite them.

Agents love fluidity and are extremely flexible. They don't mind dropping all their carefully laid plans if a better solution exists. They will change management styles and approach whenever something better comes along. But they never waver from their ultimate vision. All of the solutions, tools and initiatives Agents undertake are like chess moves. It doesn't matter which one they make, the end goal is to put you in checkmate.

Service: Thanks for calling, we'll be with you right away

There is an old story about the elevators of the Empire State Building. The tenants were complaining that the elevators were too slow. After several analyses, the engineers determined that the elevators were working as intended and there was nothing that could be done to accelerate them. One young engineer had the idea to add mirrors next to the bank of elevators. Suddenly, complaints stopped. The problem was not that the elevators were too slow, but that tenants had nothing to do during that time. Mirrors gave them an opportunity to straighten their collars and place their hairs, killing some time.

Agents understand that there are multiple facets to the service they deliver and they manage all of them. While Butlers are happy working harder and harder to provide a good service, Agents are more focused on outcomes, stopping user complaints before they arise. The Agent is the type of organization that will look for the easiest solution, such as installing mirrors.

Commercial companies in the service business organize themselves to be efficient and responsive to their customers. They use tools and processes to make the support process as smooth as possible. At the same time, they develop methods to help their customers help themselves. They simplify their products, develop self-service portals, and communities with highly engaged customers who answer questions for others (for free!). They also work very hard to set expectations ahead of time so customers will know exactly what to expect in term of speed and resolution.

Agents use the same type of approach in their own internal service world. They manage their service exactly as if it was a commercial service. In several cases, Agents have established service level agreements with its internal clients. The list of their services and expected performance goals are established and negotiated with their internal clients and used to monitor performance and report variances. This commercial-like management of their services helps them build credibility and offer the right levels of service, no more no less.

They also spend a lot of time in preventive maintenance. Agents would rather not have anyone calling in with problems. They work hard to prevent problems from happening in the first place by selecting the right products, maintaining them well and installing early warning systems. It would not be unusual for a technical support person to call a user informing them that they need to replace their computer soon as it has started issuing warnings.

People: Say hello to the next CEO

An experiment on luck was done by Wiseman. He asked different people if they were generally lucky in life. Then, they gave them a simple task: they were to count the number of pictures in a newspaper. On the second page, there was a gigantic picture written on it: "Stop counting! There are 43 pictures in this paper, report this to the experimenter." The interesting part was that the majority of the people who considered themselves lucky saw the picture and didn't have to count them at all, while the majority of the unlucky didn't see the picture and kept counting until the end. One lesson from this study is that people that perceive themselves to be lucky might simply be more attuned to opportunities that exist out there. Someone that keeps looking at the sidewalk will never see the hot blonde across the street that is looking at him. Lucky people are luckier because they see more opportunities.

Agents would be considered extremely lucky. They see opportunities everywhere. In fact, they not only see them but they actively work to create them. They use most situations to their advantage in order to move their own agendas forward.

They also regularly dip their toes outside their area of responsibility. They will frequently carve out a role as the CEO's right hand man, taking care of strategic and classified projects on his behalf. Agents will also often be assigned to lead inter-departmental projects.

Agents are often labeled as being Machiavellian. They quickly grasp the political landscape of any organization and adapt their own style accordingly. They know whose buttons to push to get initiatives approved and can block others that are in the way.

The Agent's team is also very astute. The agent isn't shy about hiring people from different industries or sectors to gain fresh insights or new methods. Agents apply commercial practices eagerly within their own environment. For example, Agents were the first to implement the business relationship management role, a liaison role between the ISP and the business that acts a little bit like a commercial account manager.

Working for an Agent can be somewhat difficult at times. The Agent is highly flexible and won't hesitate to change an orientation overnight, leaving others scrambling to keep up.

Governance: Let me see what I can do

I was once at a steering committee meeting and one of the participants jokingly said: "So Mr. Agent, what projects did you approve this year?" Everyone laughed because the intent of the meeting was to make that exact decision, yet everyone knew that the Agent had already lined up the pieces so that it would end up in a particular way.

Agents like to promote alignment by creating steering committees as governance mechanisms. These committees allow the entire company to evaluate the relative benefits of each initiative and decide which ones will get done this year. This helps promote a sense of ownership from the business as they see their projects being compared objectively and assessed on its own merits.

But of course, Agents rarely leave anything to chance. This is why they will most likely be leading the governance mechanism themselves, taking care of identifying, assessing and comparing the different initiatives on the table. Agents will also actively promote their own agenda to the rest of the business, even going so far as asking different departments to sponsor the Agent's own initiatives. The net result is that the final list of initiatives is rarely different from what the Agent wanted in the first place.

Agents also leave themselves a little bit of leeway to tackle initiatives without going through the governance mechanism. They often have a slush fund for emergencies that the use to buy favours within the business.

Budget: The Midas touch

Agents seem to have the Midas touch. Their budget is rarely scrutinized, seldom reduced and there always seem to be money available when a new initiative arises.

That's not to say that Agents are careless in their spending, quite the contrary. Agents manage their budgets tightly, ensuring that monies are properly allocated. But contrary to the Accountants, they are not on a constant quest for optimization, instead relying on being "good enough".

Agents rely on benchmarks as indicators to see if budgets are adequate. This prevents the agent from over or under spending in services and operations.

Performance measures: Protecting their reputation

Agents understand that their role as a change agent is dependent on their reputation as a service provider. If they cannot deliver the basics adequately, then no one will take them seriously. That's why the Agent measures the performance of service very seriously. Agents typically define service level agreements to set expectations around their service performance.

While most companies would report performance such as "We resolved 90% of all requests in three days." The Agent would look at it differently. They would report it as "We successfully met our service request resolution target", which would be defined in the service level agreement as being 90%. Slight difference, but it makes all of the difference in the world. The Agents don't try to achieve the best service, they try to meet targets.

Agents also try to measure their contribution to the business, but this is typically done by measuring their level of influence. This could be qualitative such as the number of major projects they are leading compared to the rest of the organization or the number of stakeholders that are supporters. Or they could be quantitative such as the ROI of their projects or the impact they have on business process performance.

But there is one metric that Agents prefer compared to everyone else: do things revolve around them. Agents like to be in control and if they sense that the organization is fully dependent on them, then they know they're succeeding.

Strategies

The Agent is a force of nature. Equally at ease in her hyper-focused area of expertise than in the industry her clients are part, she can impress just about anyone in a conversation. Very flexible, she doesn't hesitate to change strategies mid-course to adapt to new situations and events. Her intelligence, planning skills and political savviness can make her a powerful ally but also a threat to many executives, especially those that can't keep up with her. We will see three strategies to help the Agent on her quest to world domination.

1. Build trust

Agents' strength comes from their role in the business. Her unique skills and abilities makes her a strong choice for leading any type of important initiatives. But this role can quickly become a threat for others. It's not unusual to see business executives trying to send Agents back to the depth of their internal service cave.

Trust is built through consistent behaviour, something that is difficult for the hyper-flexible Agents. They can do so by making some of their work slightly more rigid so that it becomes boringly predictable. Clients love predictability, and whatever the Agent can do to become predictable will be well received.

Agents can also foster trust by making their agenda very explicit to everyone concerned. Some executives can perceive even the most well-intentioned Agent as being somewhat Machiavellian. By showing its card, the Agent can prevent people from assuming the worst.

2. Manage performance

The Agent is often out on some new exciting inter-departmental project or leading some strategic planning exercise. But this time away from operations can have some consequences, service performance slipping for example. Agents need to keep a constant focus on operational performance as it is the engine of trust with the business. Without operational excellence, the Agent will lose all credibility.

Managing performance starts with measurements. Having the right set of measures to monitor process-based performance (the work being done) and outcomes (the results from this work) is essential to ensure that everything is still in control.

Communicating this performance is also important to proactively prevent detractors from using one-time issues to undermine the Agent's credibility. As Agents become more influent, it becomes easy to see its relationship in a new light, seeing themselves as being slightly superior to everyone else and thus not needing to demonstrate its performance anymore.

3. Educate others

The agent's flexibility can be disconcerting for most people. Not everyone can understand that someone will shift its plans dramatically mid-way through execution. This can lead people to believe that the Agent doesn't have clear objectives, or that she doesn't really have a plan, that she simply improvises as she goes along.

The Agent needs to demonstrate that its objectives haven't changed, only the strategy to achieve them. And each strategy has its advantages and risks. The Agent should communicate plainly the risks involved in changing and adopting a new strategy at this stage of the initiative. While the Agent might very well be comfortable with the level of risk undertaken, not everyone shares her vision.

Working for the Agent

Working for an agent requires a great deal of autonomy. It isn't surprising to see the Agent disappear for days or weeks at a time, working on a special project for the CEO or trying a new initiative by herself. But while she is away, she expects things to carry on flawlessly. The agent spent quite a bit of time and resources developing processes to facilitate service delivery, and she expects people to follow them regardless if she is there or not. Although she likes risk and is very tolerant of big mistakes, she doesn't tolerate small errors. She expects everyone to be as professional as she is at all times. We identified three strategies to build a successful relationship with an Agent.

1. Take care of the mundane

Agents have one foot in their department and one in the business. It is not unusual for the Agent to take on external projects, such as business planning. While they are busy with these initiatives, they need to be reassured that someone is holding down the fort for them.

Taking care of the mundane means proactively managing your service so that issues and crises are detected and addressed early. Then it's simply a matter of keeping the Agent in the loop, informing her of the issue and the resolution steps you are taking. The Agent expects you to make the decisions while she is away, following the same driving principles she would use. She loves when people take initiative and would rather you'd take the wrong decision than not take any decisions at all.

2. Understand the business

Simply understanding your own area of specialty isn't enough for the Agent. She expects every employees to fully understand the business and be able to predict the consequences of any decisions on the operations. The Agent frequently uses vocabulary that is closer to the business than her own expertise, and she expects you to do the same.

The Agent has little patience to explain everything over and over again to her staff. She expects you to be autonomous and do your own homework. A good way to impress the Agent is to spend time shadowing key positions within the organization. Spend some time with the customer service team, the sales people or in the assembly plant. Understand how the business really operate, what works and what doesn't. The more aware you are of the realities on the field, the more value you will hold in the eye of the Agent. To a point where she might systematically turn to you to validate plans and decisions.

3. Don't get in the way

Much like a chess master, Agents think many moves ahead. It would be easy to jeopardize their plans by misinterpreting a directive or an action. For example, it might not be the time to pick a fight with sales if the Agent is trying to entice them to join a new initiative.

The Agent typically has little tolerance for people that barge into their chess session, much like a dog in a bowling alley. In a meeting for example, always clarify the role the Agent expects you to take and how much information she is willing to divulge. If clients asks you questions and you are not sure of the answer, wait until you can confirm with her to avoid disclosing the Agent's plan ahead of time.

The Undecided

Imagine meeting a new acquaintance. The person is friendly and outgoing. Conversation flows smoothly and is a delight to talk to. You end up sharing stories for almost an hour. The next day, you bump into the person again. Excited to chat with them, you engage the conversation but this time the person is cold, distant and boring. The next Saturday, the person calls you to meet for lunch. What's your reaction? Do you go? Chances are you'll find a polite excuse to get out of it. Most people like predictability, and dealing with someone that isn't predictable is destabilizing and uncomfortable.

The Undecided is not really a personality profile per se. Instead, it is the consequence of an ISP that is not behaving consistently with any personality profiles. Sometimes they will behave as a Nanny, sometimes as an Accountant and some days as a Butler (but rarely as an Agent).

The undecided has two major problems:

1. Inconsistent behaviour. One day the Undecided might be providing excellent customer service, the next a new priority comes in and service goes out the window. This inconsistent behaviour is a sure fire way to kill the trust relationship they could have had with their

users. In a service relationship it is critical to be predictable, so users come to trust you. But being unpredictable kills any chance of building a relationship.

The inconsistent behaviour could also come from different team members. One individual might be very customer focused while the other is more in tune with the budget. When users deal with the two individuals they don't know which one more closely represents the department's personality.

2. Says one thing, acts differently. The undecided will say that user satisfaction is very important for them (like a Butler). But in their day-to-day behaviour, they will focus on cost control like an Accountant. This is very frustrating for their users, as they are promised something and see something else entirely. But it is also very confusing for their staff as they don't know how to act. Should they do what they say or as they're doing? Like we've seen before, what interests my boss fascinates me.

By trying to please everyone you please no one
While there is no good or bad personality profile, being Undecided is definitely bad. Users don't know what to expect from them (a key factor of user satisfaction) and staff don't know how to behave. This creates confusion and miscommunication all around.

The only way to get out of this cycle is to refocus, typically by focusing on one personality profile. By focusing on one role only and doing it well, the ISP can then define its target and rebuild its credibility with the users.

Making it work

Until this point, we've look at the need for ISP to generate trust through user satisfaction, the factors that influence the role of an ISP (service and business orientation) and the four different personality profiles (Accountant, Butler, Nanny and Agent) that come from the two dimensions.

Now that you understand a little bit more about these personalities, we'll talk about how you can build a solid partnership with the business.

We'll consider a three-phase plan, starting with building credibility by making sure you don't do anything that actually breaks trust (such as providing poor service). We'll talk about the three types of alignment (team, vision, business) and finally, we'll look at ways to become a real strategic partner. Along the way we'll see what successful dieters do differently and why 63% of people that divorce are surprised by their partner's decision.

Ready?

Part 3. The Value Plan

In Part I we saw how the role of internal service providers is evolving and the importance of user satisfaction. In Part II we learned about the different ISP personality profiles. Now, we'll start to develop your plan to demonstrate your value to the business.

Building partnerships

Back when I was a CIO, one of my suppliers contacted me to schedule a meeting, having some pretty exciting news to share with me. So I scheduled the meeting and the salesperson was very happy to inform me that my company was one of their most important accounts, and they wanted to become a strategic partner to our company. I waited, expecting more but that was the news.

I could tell the salesperson had just attended a sales seminar that showcased the need for sales people to stop selling and start partnering with their clients. He was full of buzzwords and visions of how they could help our company grow and dominate the industry.

Having been a management consultant for ten years, I couldn't stop myself from asking him what being a partner would consist of exactly. My staff could see that I was leading him on, and they could barely keep themselves from laughing out loud. The sales person began to explain to me how they would sit in our strategic meetings, contributing their ideas and expertise on our industry to help us shape our orientation and direction. Keep in mind that I was working for a rendering company, a company that specializes in grinding animal carcasses into pet food. Few people outside of the industry have any expertise (or even interest) in what we do.

I made him understand that before he started considering himself a "strategic partner," he needed to start being a "decent provider." His service was fair at best, but always highly inconsistent. His invoicing had numerous mistakes, forcing us to review each invoice with a microscope. His staff were far from the brightest, and he knew nothing about our industry.

The same thing can happen with internal service providers. They start scheduling meetings with their internal clients, announcing how they intend to become their strategic partner. They begin strategic planning, gathering requirements and developing execution plans. But then things crawl to a stop. Why? Because their clients don't find them credible. As I said, "Start by delivering consistent service, then we'll talk."

Now let's look at how internal service providers can build their credibility to one day achieve the status of strategic partner.

Three steps for your Value Plan

Accelerated value creation plan:
Step 1. Deliver the Basics
Step 2. Manage alignment
Step 3. Demonstrate value

In my consulting and workshops, we develop a comprehensive assessment and execution plan for internal service providers.

While it is more effective for me to guide you through the process, this book will give you the tools you need to begin it. But it's a crash course, condensed to be used by you and your team.

Each step is designed to be completed sequentially, because they are dependent on one another. There is no point aligning your team if you are still struggling to deliver the Basics and frankly, no one will want to partner with you if you are continually in crisis management mode.

Before you begin, you need to understand that this is more than just a project. If you go through the process honestly and thoughtfully it will involve changing daily habits and making users the priority in everything you do.

I like to use the analogy of losing weight. Losing weight is extremely simple: eat less, exercise more. Yet actually doing it is extremely difficult, because you may have to change daily habits that have been in place for years (what do you mean no chips while watching TV?), and stopping impulse decisions about food. Although we are not asking you to lose weight here, be mindful of the effort that will be required.

The discussion, examples and recommendations that follow will help you and your team embark on a value journey. First, we'll look at building your credibility by delivering the Basics.

Step 1. Deliver the Basics

How credible are you as a service provider?

We've seen how the different personality profiles impact how ISPs are perceived by users and organizations. But we neglected to talk about service quality, the most critical piece of this puzzle.

In describing the personality profiles (Accountant, Butler, Nanny or Agent), we always assumed they are competent service providers. The scope and attitude toward service delivery changes from one personality profile to another, but we work with the assumption that each one delivers good service.

Even the Accountant, described as the least service and business oriented of the personality profiles, is assumed to deliver good service.

We will see in this section that delivering good base service (what we call the "Basics") is essential in building partnerships and demonstrating value.

We will look at the ISP Value Hierarchy, a model that shows the importance of delivering the Basics. We will review the user lifecycle, which are the stages users go through when using your services. We will also talk about the importance of metrics and using metrics as a diagnostic and as a driver. Finally we will talk about the different types of users.

Hierarchy of needs

Are you on the same level?

We've already talked about Maslow's hierarchy of needs. What Maslow basically said was that there are five categories of needs and they are arranged like a pyramid. You cannot fulfill higher order needs until you fulfill the most basic of needs.

The five needs are:
- Physiological: Eat, sleep.
- Safety: Have shelter, be protected from elements and threats.
- Belonging: Belong to a group, and be accepted (family)
- Self-esteem: Develop ones self.
- Self-actualization: Be the best you can be. Make a difference.

Therefore imagine for a minute that you've just lost your house to a terrible fire. Everything you cherish has been lost. Suddenly you went from an individual at Maslow's level 3 or 4 (or perhaps 5), back to being at level 1 or 2. Where will you sleep? How are you going to pay for replacing all of your belongings?

With these challenges facing you, it would certainly not be the right time for someone to approach you and ask you to take a Spanish class. Even if I had the most convincing sales arguments, you would not be in a state of mind to hear them. Your basic needs are not fulfilled, and that takes precedence over doing anything else. How is this relevant to user satisfaction?

The ISP value hierarchy

There is a similar concept called the ISP value hierarchy. Users have five categories of needs, all built on top of one another, just like Maslow. They are:

- **Access:** I have access to the basic services I need to do my job effectively.
- **Reliability:** The services are secure and available when I need it.
- **Integration:** Services are combined to become easy to use and the integration is seamless.
- **Transformation:** When the ISP provides a strategic advantage to the company.
- **Paradigm shifting:** Where the ISP the company inside out.

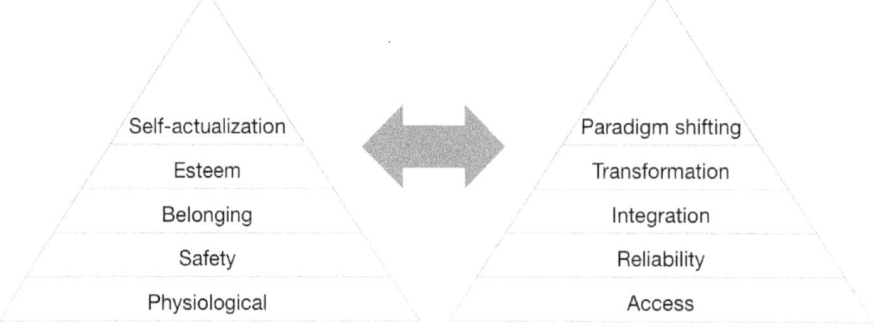

When we put these side-by-side, we realize that the ISP value hierarchy and Maslow are very similar. The first level is about having access to services. Without access to basic the resources, I can't even begin to think about how to go higher. If I don't have a decent computer with internet access and the right software, then chances are I cannot do my job effectively.

On the second level, services need to be reliable and secure. If my computer crashes regularly and I cannot rely on it, I won't be interested in learning about what it can do for me and my business. I will only use a given computer or device consistently if I can rely on it. If I couldn't rely on my car to get me from one city to another, chances are I won't be using it much. I'll take the bus or train instead. If my car dealership called me to install new leather seats, my first reaction would be to say, "Fix my car, I can't rely on it now, I'm not getting any value out of it. "

The third level concerns the integration of the services. Once levels 1 and 2 are confirmed, then I want to have the data in a convenient location so I can analyze and use the data in a seamless manner. If I have to go to three different systems to look up three different pieces of information like an order or client status then I'm not thinking about how the system can help me grow the business. If the services don't combine to facilitate my day-to-day work, chances are they will become a burden more than a benefit.

The fourth level is where we can start talking about partnerships. As a user I have access (level 1), the environment is reliable (level 2), and the services are integrated (level 3). With levels 1 to 3 in place I'm now I'm ready to discuss how I can transform my business so it runs differently. Now the ISP has a chance to be perceived as a business partner. Before the preceding levels are met it is simply a waste of time to discuss partnerships or other transformative measures.

The fifth level is where the ISP can actually use its services to turn the business around completely. At this level the ISP drives the competitive advantage of the organization through the innovative use of its services.

Jumping the gun

In our review of hundreds of strategic plans we've found that ISP becoming a partner to the business is a recurring theme. Everyone wants to help the business transform itself and play an active role in business strategy. In fact, we find that most users feel that ISPs has yet to go above level 1 or level 2. Helping the business transform itself is a level 4 or 5 conversation. There is a significant gap here. From the users' perspective, ISPs don't seem to understand anything about their own situation.

Therefore, it is important for ISPs to understand the level where users see themselves. Of course users' levels will change over time. Ten years ago mobile computing wasn't an option. Back then someone might have seen themselves at level 4; ready to discuss how IT will change everything in their business. Then tablets came out and suddenly they are back to level 1. They want tablets and need connectivity so they can be used on the road. ISPs needs to be constantly inquiring about where users stand, so they can lead the discussion about new services and orientations.

A moving target

Providing the Basics is no easy task. It requires a solid understanding of what the users truly need and having the right people, processes and tools to provide it. That in itself is enough to keep ISP leaders busy full-time. But that isn't difficult enough.

The Basics change over time. Needs evolve. Users need new services, longer service hours, new tools. Users were perfectly happy to get a desktop computer ten years ago, but now they need a laptop, an iPad and an iPhone. What was once considered Basics is now inappropriate.

But thankfully, needs also disappear. We tend to think that services should always become better and faster over time but the reality is that some services often become obsolete. An astute internal service provider will capitalize on both of these trends to keep its budget and its sanity stable by eliminating services that are no longer required.

Action items
- Identify the Basics for your service and validate with your users
- Assess if your users believe the Basics are being met (through a user survey for example)
- Continue to monitor user satisfaction with the Basics over time

What gets measured gets done

Weight loss is an interesting problem (except for those people struggling with it). It is interesting because it is done not through one single big action, but through the cumulative effect of small actions.

Daily behaviour

People struggling with weight problems have a hard time coping, because it requires them to continue doing the same thing they did before, but with greater self-control. They used to eat a lot, now they have to eat smaller portions. They used to eat dessert, now they have to skip it. They used to eat delicious, fatty food, now they need to eat bland, nutritious food.

They fight this battle every day, at every meal. And they must also fight against time constraints because it's a lot easier to pick up food at the drive-thru then it is to cook a healthy low-fat meal.

So not only do they have to fight against their nature and habits, they also have to fight against external factors like time constraints, effort, etc.

No wonder 2/3 of people who lose weight end up regaining it.

What research shows

A study published in the Academy of Nutrition and Dietetics

showed the characteristics of dieters who were able to lose and keep weight off. They've tracked dieters who lost a significant amount of weight, and then kept it off. The study was to find out the characteristics of the dieters who kept weight off versus the ones that gained it back.

Of the six characteristics identified, daily weigh-in was one of the most important. Most of the regainers said they avoided the scale out of shame or denial, or because they knew it would bring bad news. Stepping on the scale was a constant reminder of their inability to keep weight off.

Let's keep in mind these people had put in a tremendous amount of time, energy and sacrifice to lose weight in the first place. This in itself was quite an accomplishment. But most of them went back to their old ways (and old weight).

Daily behaviour requires constant feedback

Why is that? Daily weigh-in provides something that is essential to manage a behaviour: feedback.

Feedback allows us to figure out if our daily behaviours are pointing us in the right direction or not. It is easy to overeat, skip a workout session, or watch TV instead of taking a walk.

But, the knowledge that tomorrow morning you have to step on that scale is a powerful motivator. It makes eating a second dessert easier to avoid.

The worst way to wake up

Every morning I get up and head for the scale. That may seem like the worst possible way to wake up. Every morning I have a little anxiety. Is the scale going up, down, or staying the same? Of course I have a pretty good idea already what will happen, since I know what I ate and how much exercise I got the day before. But I still dread the moment. Up until I get the result. Then it is either a glorious way to wake up (I lost two pounds!) or simply a reminder to be more careful today (I gained two pounds). Either way, it's no big deal. How much weight can someone put on in a single day?

Occasionally, I will either forget or be unable to weigh myself for a few days, like when I'm travelling. Now, these are the best of times. Worry-free mornings. I wake up and I don't have this little stress waiting for me.

And it shows during the rest of the day. I'll eat without remorse and snack throughout the day. I'll eat dessert I shouldn't. And maybe I'll take it a little easier during my workout, maybe stop a little sooner because I have things to do, of course... Overall I'll just be a little bit lazier.

Unfortunately, at some point I have to get back on the scale. And my anxiety goes up. Way up. Sometimes I'm tempted to not get back on the scale ever. What if I gained five pounds? What if I gained ten pounds? As long as I don't step on the scale, it didn't happen. It isn't real yet. But the moment I step on that scale, it has happened. And at that moment I will have to deal with the results. But of course, scale or not, the pants are already aware.

It takes courage to step on the scale. It takes a lot less courage to step on the scale every day because the variations are a lot less brutal.

In this chapter we will see why measurement is a critical part of managing user satisfaction. But first, let's take a closer look at dieters and how they succeed in losing and keeping weight off.

Yearly measure doesn't work

Returning to our weight loss example, imagine if you stepped on a scale only once a year. Every January, you would starve yourself for a week, cross your fingers and step on that dusty scale. The time prior to weighing would be a period of tremendous stress, all the efforts made over an entire year summed up into one event.

But, bad news, your weight is up. Ok, no big deal, last year you fasted for two weeks before weighing yourself. And you were sick, so perhaps that helped a little bit back then. And this time you had a lot more dinner parties to attend during the holidays, so perhaps that didn't help either. And your muscles are significantly bigger, that has to count for something, right?

You can find many reasons to rationalize the weight increase that have nothing to do with the actions and strategies you took to lose weight.

No long-term focus

The same thing happens with satisfaction surveys. If you've ever been in the first meeting after the yearly satisfaction survey numbers come out, it is really something to see. Directors and VPs sit together, look at the numbers, and go through the five stages of grief:

- Denial: "These numbers don't look right, is this survey statistically valid?"
- Anger: "I told you we shouldn't have done this project in November, it's the worst possible month!"
- Bargaining: "If we remove the HR group from the survey, does that improve the numbers?"
- Depression: "These people are impossible to satisfy, we are just wasting time and effort trying."
- Acceptance: "Well, it is what it is. We'll do better next year".

And what ends up happening is that there is a lot of activity for about a month. Everyone talks about the "voice of the customer," about being "service-oriented" and doing things "right the first time." And then the first quarter budget numbers come out and everyone forgets about satisfaction. Until the next year, when the cycle starts again.

Strategy assessment

The second problem with measuring satisfaction yearly is that it's impossible to determine what helped to   improve the satisfaction. Chances are a lot happened in the year that had both positive and negative impacts on satisfaction. A project to upgrade workstations didn't go as well as planned, a new application increased productivity, the new staff on the help-desk took a little while to get up to speed. Which one of these factors had a real impact?

With a yearly survey it is impossible to know. All the factors get mashed together to form one big satisfaction number. And the problem with users is that they remember the most recent interaction and base their responses on it. So if a bad project or service occurred in the last month, chances are it will have a significant impact on the numbers.

Therefore, measuring the success of the individual elements of a satisfaction strategy becomes impossible. The managers have to "guess" which strategies were effective and which ones were not.

People are driven by metrics

Returning to our weight loss example, we can see that people are driven by metrics. It helps drive their everyday behaviour. Perhaps Patrick Lencioni said it best in his book The Three Signs of a Miserable Job, "Immeasurability" is one of the three factors of job dissatisfaction. Most employees will focus on metrics and try to beat them. But this works only as long as metrics exist.

The best example of this is financial metrics. Most companies publish financial results monthly. And they have a meeting frequency that follows the publication of financial results. The head of an ISP will probably sit down once a month with the executives and review budget numbers, explain variations and make a forecast for the coming months.

Within the departments the same thing happens with metrics concerning service quality, responsiveness, availability of infrastructure, workload, etc.

For some organizations, this meeting frequency is weekly. Regardless of the timing, satisfaction metrics should follow the same frequency. It reinforces the importance of satisfaction, to the same level as budgets.

Metrics are not only a measure of result, they are a driver
In our weight loss example, the daily weigh-in wasn't so much meant to measure weight. In fact, it is probably useless as a simple weight tracking tool. A weekly weigh-in would be more appropriate and require less effort. The real reason people weigh themselves daily is to remind them of what their priority is. This number stayed with them for the rest of the day. Every time they opened the refrigerator for a quick snack, they would think of that scale number that was higher, and close the door. Or better, they would think of their lower number and close the door even faster!

Numbers are a strong motivator and can help drive behaviour.

How a theatre measures satisfaction
I was with my wife and daughter going to a play when I saw one of the best forms of satisfaction measurement.

The play was for kids age 8 to 12. The fantastic play was about a bookstore keeper who falls in love with the chocolate-maker next door, and the ghost of the previous owner of the bookstore who helps them hurry the process along. It was funny, sweet and entertaining. Not only was it perfect for my daughter's age, it was good for adults as well. And believe me, I've seen a lot of weird children's plays, so it was refreshing to see one that wasn't new-age or just plain strange.

Leaving the theatre, two ladies were standing at a booth giving out little heart shaped buttons. They were asking people to tell them if they liked the play by putting the button in one of three boxes. The boxes were labeled "I Loved it", "It was ok", "I didn't like it." It was very simple, just put the button in the box. Being the satisfaction guy, I stopped my family and waited to see how people responded to being surveyed in this way. I was amazed to see they had 100% participation. Everyone voted, I even saw a few who voted that they didn't like the play.

It was quick, anonymous, easy and entertaining. The kids liked being asked their opinion.

The survey did some things that we all struggle to do. It was immediate, we had just gotten out of the theatre and the play was fresh in our minds. In fact, we were all still discussing it. It was simple, you only had to put the button in one of three boxes. It was compelling to people, thus the 100% response rate. For a survey it was near perfect.

It was also great in what it didn't do. Many surveys attempt to get to the heart of the issues by asking tons of questions. Not in this case. One question, did you like the play or not? If the answers were all positive, then the theatre could keep doing what it was doing. If the answers came back negative, then they would have to dig further: was it the lighting, the play itself, the comedians, the noise, the time of day, etc. This would warrant a different way and extra method to collect data, a survey or interviews for example.

The survey also did something else. First, it showed me that my opinion is important. I have no idea what they did with this feedback but I know they went to the trouble of asking for it. The second thing it did is that it provided instant feedback to cast members and employees. This kind of survey could allow them to experiment from one play to the next.

Action items
- Identify the behaviours you want to promote in your team
- Measure both process and results
- Acquire and review these metrics at the same frequency as budgets

Managing the lifecycle

The user lifecycle

Users go through a known, predictable lifecycle, typically going through five major phases:

1. **New user:** the user is just getting started using your service. In a corporate environment this typically happens when a new employee is hired. A computer and phone is provisioned, configured, delivered and setup. User accounts are created and passwords communicated to the user. The user is setup in the payroll system, and benefits are assigned.
2. **Support:** This is when the user asks for help. This will happen several times in the lifecycle of a user.
3. **Project:** This is when a user becomes part of a project (or "victim" of a project). Perhaps new software is deployed, users may have to either learn something new, or adapt their daily work.
4. **Upgrade:** This is when a service is being upgraded. It is typically something positive for the user. In IT it could be when a new computer is delivered.
5. **Departure:** This is when a user stops using the services, typically because of their departure.

Each of these phases has different characteristics in terms of expectations and anxiety. A new employee typically has a high level of anxiety but the performance requirements are typically very low; they

170

have much to learn but everyone is more accommodating. Support situations are high anxiety situations since users are not able to do their work. Upgrades are also high anxiety situations since users may fear something will break in the process ("Will I lose all my bookmarks? What about my Celine Dion mp3s?")

The level of expectation will vary based on the user's previous experience. For example, users that come from a very efficient company might be disappointed if it takes a week for their computer to be setup, while someone that comes from a small company might be amazed at getting a brand new computer. Both face the same situation, but each user will have different satisfaction levels based on their different expectations.

But one thing internal service providers consistently get wrong is the new user phase.

A first date to remember

A friend has set you up on a date with a fantastic person. They've spent days telling you how incredible this person is, how charming and polite and good looking. They even have a track record of successful relationships. In fact, the person tracks the Key Performance Indicators of the satisfaction of both parties in their relationships. More than 90% rated themselves as "very satisfied" while in a relationship with this person. So of course, your expectations are high.

You show up at the restaurant on time to meet this amazing person. Forty-five minutes later, they finally arrive. The individual sits down without saying hello and starts telling you all of the different things they will and will not do for you in a relationship. Sorry, no breakfast in bed, ever. No sharing of the remote either. The person will make breakfast, but only on Sundays. In fact, to make it easy for you the person leaves you a brochure that explains everything in detail. Finally, the person asks you to sign a sheet of paper acknowledging that you had this discussion and then leaves you to look it over and encourages you to call if you have any questions.

Does that sound romantic to you? If so, you may have spent too much time at work.

Dating at work

The reality is that a lot of first-time work impressions are made this way for new users. A new employee shows up at work, excited to start a new job and arrives at their assigned desk to find a pile of equipment and wires. A note says a technician will show up "soon" to connect everything. There is also a sheet of paper with summary instructions on how to connect to the corporate systems using the user id and passwords on the sheet. Welcome to the company!

Did on boarding ever go smoothly for anyone? Most of the time, it takes a week of back and forth with the internal service providers to get equipment setup, working and configured properly, and have the right access to applications, payroll, benefits etc.

On boarding is the very first opportunity to make a good impression on the user, but instead we typically just leave them to fend for themselves. Not what I would call a good first date.

One of my previous employer forgot to enrol me in the company's retirement plan for the first six months. When they realized their mistake, all they did as an apology was to ask me for a big check to cover my half of the pension contribution. I was not all that impressed.

Moments of truth

This is an example of a moment of truth. A moment of truth is an opportunity to improve the relationship between the user and the service provider. These are the events that can turn a dissatisfied user into a loyal fan or a new, satisfied user into an arch-nemesis. These events can also create rumours and water cooler badmouthing of a company's internal services.

Frequency is important, at first

You probably have an old friend that you talk to infrequently. Perhaps someone you grew up with. But every time you talk to him, it seems like you can just continue the conversation where you last left it. It could have been months, or years, since the last time you chatted and each time you talk it feels as natural as it ever did.

The beauty of relationships is that they get easier to maintain once they are developed. Early on, they require a lot more work. A study has shown that at the beginning of a relationship, an ISP needs to focus on contact frequency instead of contact length. As the relationship evolves, contact frequency can be replaced with longer, less frequent contacts.

ISPs can leverage these findings by adapting their interaction based on the stage of the relationship. When onboarding new users, it is important to keep interactions brief, as it is easy to overwhelm them with technical jargon and acronyms. Instead of explaining everything at once, it is better to focus on what the user will need for the next week. A client of mine had a four week onboarding process, where each week one IT representative would spend 15-20 minutes with the user to answer questions and explain what would happen in the next week. Users were thrilled, they felt supported throughout the onboarding process.

As the relationship evolves, the ISP can reduce the number of interactions with its users. For example, it can use support calls to communicate new projects and initiatives to its users, to catch their interest while they are already on the phone. Or they can focus on the client's department meeting to solicit feedback and communicate upcoming events.

Action items
- Review / design a process for onboarding new users
- Plan on frequent, short interactions early on, and less frequent interactions later
- Develop a communication plan for the entire user lifeycle

Understanding the users

One size doesn't fit all

Internal service providers get economies of scale by standardizing their service across departments and users. After all, if someone needs a computer or payroll services, chances are the same computer and payroll service will work for everyone else. By reducing the number of devices to manage, or customization to maintain, we simplify service delivery and make it more productive and less-expensive.

Users don't all have the same needs. But most ISPs structure their service in a one-size-fits-all mode. The reality is that some users are looking for a turn-key solution in which they don't have to do anything, while others want the bare minimum since they already know what they want and are knowledgeable. Treating these users the same as you treat everyone else is guaranteed to cause dissatisfaction.

So while service providers want to maintain uniformity in the solutions and equipment it provides, it can certainly adapt its services to users' expectations, needs and knowledge.

Let's look at two examples of users with very different needs: the late adopter who has very little interest in your services and the early adopter who could perhaps teach you a thing or two.

Late adopter: Just make it work

The late adopter really doesn't care what's inside the box. He just wants it to work. The late adopter is not interested in how things work, what caused a problem or how you made it work again. He just wants to move on with his life.

How do you serve the late adopter? First, by fixing his issue as quickly as possible. The late adopter asks for support or help at the very last minute. He waited /procrastinated as long as he possibly could because he didn't want to deal with the problem, perhaps hoping that it will fix itself or disappear on its own over time. So by the time the late adopter reaches out, the problem has already become a crisis. Now is not the time to try to educate him on what he did wrong or how he could resolve the problem by himself.

Once the problem is fixed it is a good opportunity to follow-up with him to make sure the problem has indeed been resolved. You can take this opportunity to slowly begin educating him, hopefully to generate a level of interest, or at least make him less distrustful of your services.

The power user: Knows exactly what she wants
The power user is the kind of user that will call you with a very specific request. Perhaps they want a specific headset to use for taking calls while on the computer. They want their payroll deductions adjusted by exactly this amount to compensate a changing financial situation.

Power users know a lot about the services you provide. They may be a real specialist, trained and educated in your area of expertise or enthusiasts who spend a lot of time learning by themselves. Either way, they are very knowledgeable, and specific in what they want.

How do you annoy power users? Easy, force them to go through the same support process as everyone else. One of the best examples of power users is in the IT world. Most people have computers at home and many are actually quite good at maintaining and even building their own equipment. Younger power users who build specialized computer workstations for gaming tend to know the subtle differences between the types of memory, CPUs and graphic cards that go into a computer system. They also understand the role drivers and system settings have on performance, continually tweaking their own systems to gain a slight advantage over their opponents.

When a power user calls the IT help-desk for a problem with their workstation, they don't want to go through the same routine of questions as everyone else. Not only is it a waste of their time, they actually find it insulting. "Is the computer plugged in? Can you verify please? Is the green light showing? Is the monitor open?". This process of elimination that works well for most users is an insult to power users.

Internal service providers that recognize these kinds of differences can adapt their services to reflect the knowledge level of their users. In some cases, their expertise can even be leveraged to extend the reach and effectiveness of the internal service provider staff by developing embedded experts, which can be very useful when an ISP has several locations to cover, and not enough staff to do so. Power users can also be used as members of user groups, to help identify upcoming trends and needs regarding the ISP services.

Action items
- Identify the different types of users and their needs
- Adapt service delivery based on the expertise of the user
- Include power users in your service delivery process

Summary - Deliver the Basics

The first step of the action plan is concerns building credibility by delivering Basic services.

1. **Make sure users receive the Basics** - Without the Basic services they need, users will never be able to climb the ISP value hierarchy and allow you to take a more strategic role. Basics vary by service, by organization and over time. Therefore, it is important to constantly communicate with users to understand their expectations.

2. **Measure** - Measuring satisfaction allows you to determine if you are delivering the Basics, and helps drives your team. Continual feedback demonstrates the importance of user satisfaction, and helps identify which initiatives work and which don't.

3. **Manage the lifecycle** - Users goes through different lifecycle phases (from onboarding to leaving the organization). Each phase has different requirements and importance. Onboarding is consistently missed by internal service providers, as perhaps the best time to make a good first impression.

4. **Understand your users** - ISPs have different types of users, from the occasional user to the power user who may understand your service as well as you do. Instead of offering a

one-size fits all service where everyone is disappointed, adapting your service to different user segments can increase satisfaction dramatically.

Step 2. Manage Alignment

Are you aligned?

Alignment is a popular topic in business literature these days. It seems you can't open a business magazine that doesn't include something about how ISPs need to align with their businesses. Everyone seems to agree about its importance and how the future of ISPs and organizations depend on it.

But few seem to understand what alignment really means.

The second step of the Value Journey consists in aligning your team with the needs of the business. But as we'll see, there are three types of alignment to be mindful of.

Governance is part of alignment, but alignment is not just governance.

Something I like doing is browsing job descriptions for ISP leadership positions. Some clients have even asked me to help them write a description for upcoming vacancies. One thing that they always want to include is, "Align the service with the needs of the business." Then I ask, "How will you know when someone is aligned?" and the answer is almost always the same "When I feel they are working alongside me." That sounds pretty hard to measure.

Business literature talks a lot about alignment and nearly always focus on governance. I agree that governance is an important part of alignment. If the right processes and mechanisms aren't in place to drive the decisions of the business then it is difficult to say we are aligned.

Intuitively we all know what being aligned means. But try to explain it to a 9 years old kid. Difficult, right? It turns out that alignment is actually a scientific concept and can be measured.

As we said, alignment includes more than governance. Alignment is impacted by 1) service orientation (the importance of customer service in an ISPs day-to-day operations) and by 2) business orientation (the level of influence the ISP has on the business).

Alignment has not one dimension, but three. In this section we will talk about 1) alignment within the ISP team (team alignment) 2) alignment between the team and the leader's vision (vision alignment) and, 3) alignment between the team and the business (business alignment).

Team alignment

Alignment within the team

ISPs and their employees are easy to stereotype. "Finance people only care about budgets." "The guys in IT don't want to pick up the phone!" "HR spends their day talking."

But the reality is that each department consists of individuals that may or may not have the same values and behaviours. Chances are the individuals have different perspectives on what the role of the department actually is.

I was doing a workshop with an ISP and we came to the section about the role of the department. The leader told me in no uncertain terms, " I don't think we need to spend any time on this, it's pretty obvious to everyone that we are here to ..." and then someone cut him off to say, "Sure, we all know we need to cut costs as much as possible." And the shocked leader looked at him and said "That isn't it at all!" Turns out we needed to spend time on the department's role after all.

Teams have their own personality profiles. Their personality is shaped by their natural attitudes, their previous experience and what they believe to be the priority of their ISP. But of course personalities differ from one person to another. Some might believe their mission is to deliver a service at the lowest cost (an Accountant), while others think users are clueless and need strong guidance (a Nanny).

Personality differences will be seen in their behaviours and actions.

If the team isn't aligned, it becomes a problem for the users. How many users refuse to call the helpline, choosing instead to call individuals directly? They do so because they know that not all agents on the helpline share the same personality and they want to be sure they speak to someone they can relate to. When users start believing the ISP is fragmented, they start doubting its effectiveness.

Users like predictability, and a misaligned ISP is not consistent in providing service. One agent will be keen to help, while another will try to close the call as soon as it can. When fragmentation happens clients no longer know what to expect, a surefire recipe to let expectations go wild and cause dissatisfaction.

This lack of team alignment can also cause team conflict. Team members will disagree on the orientation to use in a given situation or initiative, since they don't share the same vision of service. Some will want to dictate their views on users and do the project rapidly, while others will believe they need to actively involve the users in the solution and take their time. These differences in vision can lead to major conflicts.

When one member of the team isn't aligned with the others

The IT department of a retail company has seen tremendous change in the past year. IT wasn't able to build a relationship with the business, and the other departments were distrustful. IT was behaving like a Pseudo-Nanny, it didn't understand the business sufficiently to provide real value. The IT meetings became confrontational, and IT was excluded from all major important decisions. The leader was fired and a someone new brought in to realign the organization.

The first year was filled with activity. People were let go and others hired. The new leader worked hard to communicate his vision for the department, which stressed being more Butler and less Nanny. It was their only choice since most of the new people in IT didn't come from the retail world and had little business knowledge. But the new people knew plenty about managing services and satisfying users.

The entire team refocused on this new vision except for one person: Bob, the old right-hand man. Bob was the second in command when the previous leader was in place. But Bob didn't see the new vision and practices as an improvement. To him, it was like saying that all he the work he had done for the past ten years was garbage. So Bob had a hard time changing his attitude and behaviour, in fact he didn't change his behaviours at all and his attitude became worse.

Bob openly criticized others in team meetings, and would point out why projects or initiatives "won't work." He would talk condescendingly about users who needed new equipment saying, "Why? They won't know what to do with it." Bob thought he knew how the business should be run and was ready to make it happen, whether the users wanted it or not.

It came to a point where his colleagues didn't want him as part of the team, excluding him from important meetings and decisions. Users didn't want to deal with him, cancelling meetings or simply not showing up.

Bob was a Nanny living amongst Butlers. Extreme opposites in both service and business orientation.

When an entire team isn't aligned
The finance department of a manufacturing company had gone through centralization, consolidating several regional offices into its headquarters building. Rather than relocating people, the department decided to let the regional employees go and hire new staff at headquarters, a decision that angered a lot of employees.

By coincidence, several of the key leaders that were hired all came from the same company. This previous employer had some very strong processes and business practices in place, something the finance department wanted to improve in the coming years. They felt that hiring these people with experience working in a more mature environment would help drive the organization forward in the right direction.

Unfortunately, there was a culture clash almost instantaneously. The finance team already in place had a Butler personality (wants to help) while the new hires were mostly Nanny (tells users what to do). As soon as the new leaders started emitting new directives or processes, the old team would complain about how it is unfair for users and how it would damage their already difficult relationship with the business. However, the new hires felt the old team allowed too many exceptions preventing automation of the processes, and producing additional manual labor.

The CFO, leading the finance team, was stuck between both departments. He wanted to deliver a good service like a Butler, but was under a Board directive to tighten financial processes like a Nanny. The CFO had a hard time establishing a clear directive for finance and the department became an "undecided", a department without focus, which severely impacted their credibility and their relationship with the rest of the business.

How do we fix team alignment issues?
Fixing team alignment issues is not an overnight process. It takes time and effort. But it is an essential task.

There are three main phases to fix team alignment issues:

1. Recognize there is an issue
Team alignment issues can be difficult to recognize. Is it an alignment issue or is someone being a jerk? Or is it because they don't share the same priorities due to their role? For example, a project

manager will have a different focus than an operational manager. It's just the nature of their job.

The good thing about alignment is that it can be measured. By evaluating the entire team on their service and business orientation, it becomes easy to see how aligned (or unaligned) the team actually is. Measurement can also highlight individuals that don't share the team's vision.

2. Provide specific guidance on desired behaviours

Once a team alignment issue has been recognized, it's time to make some tough decisions. The first is to determine if the team members who aren't aligned with the others have the potential to become aligned. This determination can lead to hard decisions such as transfers or even terminations. Isn't it better to identify these early on than allowing them to possibly pollute the work environment?

Specific guidance will need to be given to people that need to change their personality profile. People that have acted as a Nanny all of their professional lives may very well be able to become a Butler, but what does that mean for them on a day-to-day basis? People can change from one personality profile to another, but it takes a lot of daily effort and communication since the new profile may not be natural for them.

3. Reinforce the desired behaviours frequently

Some of my clients use the personality profile terminology in their day-to-day interactions. For example, I would frequently hear someone in a meeting say, "Stop acting like a Nanny!" Using the profiles helps to set expectations of desired behaviours. When people begin acting like their old selves, you can remind them they are not acting as the correct personality profile.

Action items

- Evaluate personality profiles of your key team members

- Assess alignment of the team
- Aggressively address individuals not aligned
- Positive reinforcement to those individuals in alignment

Vision alignment

Alignment with the vision

Do you sometimes feel like you are speaking Chinese to your staff? You explain what to do and then they go back to their desks and do something completely different? If that's the case you may be suffering from vision alignment issues.

One of the greatest challenges for leaders with a new group is communicating and executing a vision for how things should be.

Often, leaders have to fight against years of ingrained behaviours and habits. They have to undo a lot of old patterns. All while reassuring staff that the new vision doesn't imply that everything else prior to this day was wrong.

Sometimes these people don't agree with the new vision. When I worked at IBM there was an expression used commonly when a leader came in with a new idea: "We'll just wait him out." Leaders come and go and people know that if they wait and resist long enough, the new leader will be replaced with someone else with different ideas.

Leaders are also guilty of saying one thing and doing something else. There is an expression that says "What interests my boss fascinates me." Leaders often talk about the need for great customer service but on a daily basis they worry a lot more about crises and budgets. What people remember are not the big ideas and orientations but rather the smaller day-to-day behaviours that drive decision-making.

Again, using the concept of service and business orientation it is easy to measure and identify issues with vision alignment. A team that has a completely different personality profile from their leader is easy to spot.

Misalignment example: Butlers that must act as Accountants

An ISP for a public-sector organization was struggling with their service delivery. They hired us to assess their service delivery and figure out what wasn't working and why, and correct the situation.

This ISP used to have a great relationship with its internal clients. Previously the clients had controlled the budget for projects and were therefore used to get pretty much everything they wanted. The ISP would staff up based on clients' needs and deliver accordingly. But then the executives decided to centralize budgets for projects and let the ISP manage it, reducing them drastically in the process.

The project staff tried to make do with the reduced budget. Everyone picked up a little more work, worked longer hours. Clients continued to request projects and the staff tried to accommodate them by finding innovative ways to deliver. But the staff couldn't create more hours in the day, and creativity can only go so far, so projects started falling behind.

As time went by, projects were delayed more and more up to a point where only half of the projects agreed upon were completed. Clients were furious with the delays. The project staff was exhausted, several having left due to burn-out. People were trying to transfer out of the department. The relationship with the business was at an all-time low, and the department had lost all of its hard earned credibility.

When we started doing the assessment, the problem became clear very rapidly. The project staff were seeing themselves as Butlers, the role they played for many years. But now their leader was asking them to change their role and become Accountants. The organization couldn't afford to spend as much as they used to and needed to cut back significantly. But the project teams didn't know how to behave like Accountants.

How to correct vision alignment issues

Vision alignment is easier to correct than team alignment. The reason is simple: one person creates most of the problem. Yes, that's right, if your team isn't aligned with your vision, it means you are probably the problem.

Now, team alignment also happens when a new leader arrives, bringing new ideas, perspectives and values. But the good news is that the leader holds all the cards needed to fix the situation.

First step: Are you the problem?

Are your communications clear? I'm talking about how and what you communicate to your team when it comes to service delivery. It is important to remember that communication happens by other means than talking. If your vision and daily behaviour collide, then yes, you are the problem. Your actions speak louder than your voice. If you talk about being user focused but you yourself never visit the front line and talk to the staff, you're sending the wrong message. It's critical to lead by example.

Second step: Do people understand?

Do people understand what specific behaviours you expect of them? It's easy to say "Be customer focused" but what does it mean when I'm back at my desk? Do you communicate what you expect in terms of daily behaviour? Do you provide ongoing training and examples of how to interact with users? Do you provide examples of good and bad reactions to common situations? These are all important elements of clear communication of your vision. It's easy to talk about grand theories, but daily behaviours will make sure the team really understands what you expect from them.

Third step: Do you enforce it?

Modifying behaviours is one of the most difficult things a leader has to do. It requires constant vigilance to prevent the old behaviours from resurfacing. Leaders need to constantly monitor and enforce their vision, even on days when they just don't feel like it.

A client of mine had a disorderly and messy tech support group. Computers were everywhere. I told him that in order to raise credibility he had to enforce some sort of discipline on his staff. Every month I went back, the tech area was still messy. The leader said, "I asked a few times for them to clean it up but then I got tired of repeating it, I'm not a baby-sitter." What he did instead is that he showed his team that if they ignore requests long enough they would go away.

Values are important only if you stick to them when it hurts. It requires a personal commitment and daily efforts to maintain this level of discipline.

Action items
- Communicate your vision clearly
- Define expectations in terms of daily behaviours
- Enforce the new vision every day
- Follow-through

Business alignment

Alignment with the business

Industry magazines often have articles on how HR, IT or finance need to "align" with the business in order to be successful.

This trend will likely last a while. A study conducted by the Harvard business review showed that more than 50% of CEOs were disappointed with their internal service providers. They felt that the ISPs "didn't get it", that they were a commodity within their organization. The CEO also expected major changes in the future for IT leaders and departments.

In the IT world there was a major trend to have the chief information officer (CIO) report to the CEO. Studies by predicted that more than 50% of CIOs would report to the CEO within the next five years. What has happened instead has been the exact opposite. As CIOs began reporting to CEOs, the CEO saw very quickly that the CIOs weren't "getting it." That trend has now reversed (and a bunch of CIOs got fired) and now CIOs tend to report to finance instead, changing its role from value creator to cost centre.

The lack of alignment between the CEO and the CIO became obvious to the CEO. In many cases, CIOs were unable to keep up and were unable to be the partner the business wanted. IT leaders were preoccupied with technology and costs (being Accountants) while the CEO wanted and needed an Agent to help transform the business. In some cases, they even expected a Nanny to take control and drive change throughout the organization.

This scenario happened in several areas, not just IT, but also HR, finance, logistics. Business alignment is critical for the success of the internal service provider.

Controlling shipments

The regulatory group of a shipping company centralized all of its operations into one office, eliminating positions at various warehouses. The objective was to reduce costs, harmonize business practices, and reduce the number of shipping infractions, by hiring more skillful and knowledgeable people, who had the correct shipping certifications.

The shipping regulatory department is responsible for identifying and providing the paperwork required to ship controlled goods across the country and over international borders. Their role is extremely important since that paperwork ensures that proper safety measures are taken whenever a shipment of goods is made. They also help governments protect their borders by ensuring that the goods shipped aren't in violation of environmental laws. This process requires understanding the laws and regulations of dozens of countries and the specifications of thousands of chemicals, which is not an easy task.

In the past, warehouse managers were responsible for this process, which resulted in hundreds of thousands of dollars in penalties for violating key shipping laws and requirements. The decision was made to centralize the group when one of the company's warehouses nearly lost its shipping permit due to a major blunder.

Warehouse managers used to have someone trained in shipping regulations sitting right next to them at the warehouse. Calling the central office to speak to the regulatory group was not a reflex for them. So what happened is that the regulatory group got warehouse requests at the last minute, forcing them to work overtime and cut corners. In some instances, they even had to delay shipping since not all paperwork had been completed. The regulatory group wanted to position themselves as an Agent, but it was clear that was not the direction they were headed.

How to fix business alignment issues

Fixing business alignment issues requires ISP leaders to have alignment inside the team, and to also have alignment with the leaders' vision. Without this alignment, the team will not act consistently and any attempt to fix business alignment will be a waste of time and worsen the situation.

Leaders can fix business alignment issues by following a three-phase approach:

1. Identify the source of alignment issues

Internal service providers like to refer to whatever is outside of their department as "the business." But the reality is that the company consists of individuals and departments which may have different ideas of what the role of the ISP should be. Once you understand what the different expectations are, you can begin to determine why these variations in expectations are happening. Are their needs different? Do they understand the role you can play?

2. Communicate what you can and cannot do

Business alignment issues often arise from users having unrealistic expectations of the services you can offer. Users would like for your services to be available 24/7, but the reality is that your budget only allows normal business hours. By communicating your service standards (what you will and what you can't do) and the reasoning behind them (cost, regulation, standards, usefulness, etc.) you help users understand the realities of your service delivery.

3. Change expectations

The next step to fixing business alignment issues is to start shaping expectations. Perhaps your users don't understand that you can contribute original ideas to their operations. By proposing ideas, you demonstrate that you understand their realities and that you are knowledgeable of their industry, which gives you credibility and perhaps causes them to see you differently. This can help users better understand your potential contributions and involve you in strategic discussions.

Action items

- Assess the expectations of the different business stakeholder groups
- Identify gaps between their expectations and your current personality profile
- Communicate your service-level performance targets to set the correct expectations

Step 3. Demonstrate Value

What does it mean to be a partner?

What's the biggest difference between a supplier and a partner? Simply put, the partner doesn't wait for you to ask for something in order to do it.

The partner anticipates your needs and makes sure they are met exactly when you need them. A partner needn't be told to improve their service levels; they know where their service levels stands based on user feedback. Partners respond to the needs of their clients, and adapt service and behaviour to meet their clients' emerging demands.

Being a partner is a two-way street. The partner can ask their clients to change their behaviour, to help the partner when needed. In a partnership, neither partner is shy about telling the other when they are doing something wrong.

A partnership really succeeds when both parties are committed to meeting the same objectives. It takes an incredible amount of trust for a partnership to succeed, which is why workable, long-term partnerships are so rare.

In this section we will see how you can become a proactive partner.

Manage satisfaction

Satisfaction drives value

We've seen earlier how satisfaction helps internal service providers drive value. Business executives have very little interest in what you do, except for how it affects their business. Executives don't understand the complexities you face in delivering service, so they are not accurate evaluators. Therefore, they rely on the next best thing: the satisfaction of their employees. If their employees are happy with your service, then chances are you are delivering value. But if their employees are not satisfied, they will assume you are not delivering value and no amount of ROI calculations will convince them otherwise.

The goal of step 3 is to manage the value the organization receives from your services. And a key element of value is managing satisfaction. While delivering excellent service is a critical element, we will also see how managing expectations, reducing your users' anxiety and handling complaints are also important.

Service matters more than skills

There is no doubt; delivering services requires a high level of technical expertise. ISP staff face a wide variety of issues dealing with the different parts of their services. In many cases they must guess what the user did to cause the problem. The job requires strong technical skills as well as good deduction and forensic capabilities. That's why most support personnel are people who have strong

197

technical backgrounds.

But if we consider that ISP support is really a service business, then are technical skills the only skills we need?

How often have you heard your IT support staff joking about a user that used a cd drive as a coffee holder (did this really happen?) or that a user tried to plug a cable into the wrong outlet? I had a colleague I used to tease because he would consistently plug the computer cable into the projector upside down, forcing it in to make it fit. So the cables always had crooked pins, and we consistently had a colour missing from our presentations.

Approach is more important than skills

Researchers tried to determine what's more important for users: technical or customer service skills? They've conducted evaluations and surveys to understand the things that make service encounters satisfying for users. Technical skills came out as important (15%), obviously. At the end of the day the problem needs to be fixed. But service skills rated twice as high (27%). This means that the approach agents use to resolve the problem, and their attitude, is more important than how they fix the problem.

Keep in mind that for a novice user, technical skills quickly become a blur. It is much like for me, there is no difference between a good artist and a master artist. To me they are all very good and I can't differentiate between artists because I'm too clueless about art and art techniques. A knowledgeable person might see subtleties in paint strokes, the use of colour, or the composition of the painting, but for me it's all the same.

The same is true for many users. For them, ISPs are difficult beasts and their knowledge level is very limited. So the difference between a complete novice and a very competent person are sometime difficult to differentiate. A very competent person might diagnose the problem

198

a bit sooner, and would have to take fewer steps to fix it. But for a user this difference might be invisible.

But, the thing I will remember as a user is how the agent talked to me and made me feel about the problem. If the agent was rude or complacent then I would definitely be displeased about the interaction, even if it solved the problem. Users may not understand the technicalities, but they know when they are getting bad service.

We don't train for service

Recognizing that the approach is twice as important as skills, you would expect ISPs to provide twice as much training on support competencies, right? Wrong. Most ISPs perform no training on how to provide service, and there are a couple of wrong reasons why they don't:

* We need all the training just to keep up with the technology trends
* Attitude can't be trained

Even the most attentive and empathetic support agent may do things to annoy users without realizing it. It could be describing issues as so easy the user should have fixed them, or hurriedly fixing a problem. These types of behaviour can be fixed by appropriately training the agents on how to interact with users.

I don't mean using bland, script-driven nonsense we see in call centres all over the world. The idea is not to sterilize service encounters and make users feel they are talking to a machine, but instead to emphasize what's it like for a user to solicit help.

Users feel much anxiety when faced with an issue since the very item that isn't working keeps them from doing their work and meeting their deadlines. The user may already have spent time trying to fix the problem and failed, so besides anxiety they are probably feeling frustration too. Recognizing how the user may be feeling is essential in providing service.

Managing anxiety is the name of the game. Whatever the agent can do to emphasize that they are there to help, and that they will see the problem through to resolution, and ensure users they will soon be back to their work will help to give the user assurance and help to calm them. Recognizing the user's state of mind and showing empathy can do wonders for user satisfaction.

Service delivered VS service expected

One of the key elements of satisfaction is the difference between the service that users expect and the service they do receive.

Managing expectations

Expectations change depending on what was promised and what our past experience has been. Let's look at fast food, a business that promises very fast service. They are promising us that we will be able to get in, order quickly and get our food quickly, eat and get on with our day. That's the entire premise of fast-food: a quick meal. If I want a good meal, I will go elsewhere.

Users have the same kinds of expectations. When I have an issue, I expect someone to answer the phone quickly (within 5 rings) to diagnose my problem without making me feel stupid, and to provide a solution so I can get back to work. Depending on my past experience I may have different expectations. For example, I know changing hardware can take some time, because IT doesn't carry inventory. Or that ordering a mouse requires two days of internal approvals. But I do have an idea of what to expect.

Tell the users what to expect

The first step in managing expectations for an IT department is to tell its users what to expect. Similar to how a restaurant advertises its qualities (fast, fresh, free toy!), ISPs can also advertise what users should expect.

The easiest way to do this is by developing and publishing a service level agreement (SLA). A SLA is basically a list of promises that ISPs make to the organization and its users. It should include items like:

- We will answer the phone within 5 rings 90% of the time
- We will be available from 8:00am to 5:00pm Monday through Friday
- We will provide support on weekends within four hours

These promises are an attempt to set expectations. By explicitly telling users that you are committing to this, I now know what you can do for me. Just like the restaurant analogy, I now know what you are promising. You'll answer most phone calls within 5 rings. You are available from 8:00am to 5:00pm, so if I call between these hours I know you will answer and help me out.

Equally important though is that an SLA can advertise what ISPs cannot do. It tells the user "we will answer the phone within 5 rings, but not if you call after five and not on the week-ends." So the users that call at 6:00 p.m. will know they won't get an immediate response. Users might not be happy about it but they would know what to expect.

SLAs establish the characteristics of the service delivered. Understanding the boundaries of what ISPs can and cannot do creates a new set of expectations for the user. But past experiences can throw this out the window.

The role of past experiences

The last time I went to a fast-food place I had the most amazing burger. For some reason it was one of the best I've ever had. Perhaps it was because the cook was particularly good, or the food was very fresh, or perhaps I was starving and anything would have tasted good. But my last experience there was fantastic. Unfortunately, this last encounter was problematic. Now when I go to this particular restaurant, I expect the same burger.

Few fast food chains promise that the food will be outstanding. They promise fresh, hot, or something along those lines, but they never promise your life will be transformed by the culinary experience they provide. They know they cannot deliver that kind of service. Too expensive, too complicated, not scalable at the level they need, and not fast enough. Delivering an amazing meal was never their promise.

So the next time I ate a burger I was disappointed. It wasn't as fresh and delicious as the one I'd had before. I expected something better. It wasn't bad; it wasn't even different from the last hundred times I've been there. But it was different from my last experience. That last experience had changed my expectation of the service I would receive.

The same thing exists in ISPs. You can broadcast to your users that you will not pick up the phone, or that all requests must be sent via email. You've established your SLA, you've tried to set expectations: don't contact us by phone. It can't be any clearer. Yet, the ISP employees keep answering the phones. They are nice people, they don't want to disappoint the users, so they keep answering the phones and solving issues.

So as a user, I've discarded the expectations that you've tried to set through your SLA because you answer the phone. I now expect you to answer the phones all the time. The last time I called you answered the phone, I don't see why it should be different this time. This is where trouble starts. Because the next time I call, you may not answer. You were busy, or not at your desk. I have always had someone answer my calls, but now I don't. After 4 hours, I get a call back from the ISP, with the person apologizing because the department was in a meeting all day and couldn't answer the phones. I am frustrated because I've been waiting four hours. The ISP employee is frustrated because he has been doing me a favour by answering the phone when I call. This service encounter leaves everyone disappointed.

This is why it is important to deliver what's promised and be consistent about it.

Better living through ISPs

We've seen that a major source of dissatisfaction is the anxiety users have toward technology. They are bombarded with new technologies every day at work and at home. They may feel they cannot cope with the amount of information they must retain, just to keep up.

If you've setup a home theatre system recently you understand what I'm talking about. Chances are you have four or five remotes sitting on your coffee table. Some might only be used to actually turn on a certain device. But you do need to remember to change the input on the TV, turn on the DVD player and turn on the home theatre system and set the components at the right inputs. At my house the home theatre became a source of stress. I would hear yelling and frustration, and then I would go down to the basement and explain for the Nth time that you have to turn on the devices in a specific order or the system won't work correctly.

After explaining all that for the millionth time I gave up. I bought a universal remote. I programmed only what we needed and removed everything else. So now we only have a handful of options: watch TV, watch a movie. That's it. My family is thrilled, they can now use the equipment without a 200-page user manual and I don't have to provide home theatre support anymore. What I've effectively done is reduce the anxiety of my users (my wife and daughter) by allowing them to do something that used to be easy: watch TV. Their techno-stress used to be through the roof as they felt incompetent in front of the new equipment and they even exhibited avoidance behaviour ("forget it, I'll read a book instead"). The training I gave didn't work effectively in this case since they had little interest in learning the entire home theatre ecosystem and didn't felt like exploring. With the addition of a new technology (the universal remote), we simplified the entire process by automating tasks and eliminating options.

This process of simplification actually allowed my users to benefit more from the technology.

Too many options are bad

A study by Iyengar analyzed the behaviour of customers who were presented with different numbers of choices. They ran an experiment where people walking by were asked to buy different kinds of jam. One group of subject chose between six different types of jams, while another group chose between 24 types of jam. Now, you'd think more choice would be better right? Well, the results showed something else entirely. The subjects that had to choose between 24 choices actually chose NOT to buy anything. Of those who chose between 6 items, most chose one. The higher number of choices actually had the effect of paralyzing those subjects.

Hide options

Computer systems have become increasingly complex with hundreds or thousands of options. If you look at everything word processing software can do, it is staggering. It can manage small databases of addresses, it can create web pages, and it can make promotional materials of all sizes and lengths. It is an incredibly useful tool in the hands of someone that is highly trained. But it is overkill for someone who simply wants to write a letter. The number of options actually makes the task more difficult to do.

Word processors have a clever way of limiting that complexity, they hide the options. Options are buried under menus, contextual menus, ribbons, etc. and are grouped together based on the task you want to do.

The same can be done with other software. I'm always surprised at the number of packages that are deployed as-is, without any simplification of the interface for the non-expert users. Figuring out what different levels of functionality different users need and hiding the rest can make a big difference in the user experience.

Add technology where it makes sense

Sometimes simplification comes from adding technology. The same way that I added a universal remote, ISPs can add software to aggregate data or to make software more readily available. For example, companies have used intranets for years to make systems available to users. This is especially useful for tasks that users might do only once in a while (expense reports, yearly performance reviews, etc.).

Complaint department

Communication is an exchange that has three parts--the message, the medium and the feedback. If all I'm doing as an ISP is sending messages without giving a way for users to respond, then I'm not communicating, I'm advertising.

We often mix up advertising and communication. Sometimes we feel that if we send emails, we publish articles in the company newsletter or hold teleconferences, that we're doing a good job communicating. But good communication must provide a way for users to respond.

A study pointed out that in order to feel satisfied; users must be able to voice their concerns. Without a way to voice concerns, all they can do is complain among themselves which causes others to have the same concerns. Satisfied users will generally tell two people, while dissatisfied users will tell 10 or more people.

In order to improve customer satisfaction we must do the following:

1. Provide a platform

A suggestion box or complaint hotline is a great way to provide such a soapbox to the users, giving them a way to voice their concerns.

As a CIO, I always provided my phone number, cell phone and email in all communications. I asked people to reach out to me directly if they had any issues or concerns. At first people were worried that I would be swamped with complaints, but in reality I generally got less than one email or phone call a week. Each time I received a message I would call the user back, ask exactly what happened, then log into the ticket support system to see what had been done. Then I would figure out what it would have taken to resolve the issue to the user's satisfaction. I would then use this as a way to teach the IT staff how to satisfy users, either by being more attentive to the users' real problem or by ensuring that the issue had indeed been resolved. It worked wonders since users felt they had a bat-phone to call in case of trouble. It also worked well for the IT staff since they saw I wouldn't crucify them with the information from complaints but would diligently make sure the problem was addressed and use it as a learning experience.

2. Follow-through

The second step is to follow through with the complaint. To experiment I've visited other company's web sites that had a "How did we do, tell us!" type of button to see how effective they are in dealing with customer complaints. I would leave a message that I was less than happy. I was shocked at the sheer number of companies that never called or emailed me back. More than half of companies I contacted never responded except for an auto-reply that stated something along the lines of "Thanks for your email; we take your satisfaction very seriously. We will analyze your request and get back to you shortly." And those that did respond seemed less interested in fixing the issue than they were in up-selling or cross-selling something to me.

What about the companies who did respond? Some of them had someone senior call me back, apologize, and genuinely attempt to identify the problem, try to fix it and thank me for my patience.

In marketing we call this service recovery. We already know that few people actually complain, people that have problems usually vote with their feet, as in go elsewhere. Thus each complaint is actually very precious and should be treated as such. It's an opportunity to right a wrong and actually build a deeper relationship with the customer. And studies have shown that a user whose service was eventually recovered had a very high level of satisfaction, even if the original contact did not satisfy them. Knowing that the company tried and succeeded in fixing the issue increases the likelihood they would buy from the company again.

ISPs face the same issues. When users are dissatisfied with our service they have nowhere else to go, so they can't vote with their feet. But they will feel dissatisfied. This is why every complaint is a chance to right a wrong, or to fix an issue that happened in our service delivery. But it only works if we follow-through. If a service email doesn't get answered for days, or gets re-routed in the ticket system to be opened by the same agent again, it won't create satisfaction.

This is why following through with every complaint is essential. Since ISPs cannot get new "clients", it must make sure that all the current clients (users) are satisfied, and service recovery is the way to keep them satisfied.

3. Be transparent
What are three phrases you never hear in an ISP?
1. "No thanks, we have more than enough money in the budget, we don't need more"
2. "Microsoft makes some fine software"
3. "Oh wow, looks like we screwed up big time. Here, let me fix it."

An important element of user satisfaction is trusting the company.

Too often we hide behind jargon and the complexity of ISPs to hide our mistakes. Some go so far as insinuating it is the user's fault when there are problems ("oh, looks like you streamed some music, that's what erased your entire hard drive"). But the reality is that ISPs screws up. Regularly. There are good and bad reasons for it, but at the end of the day we screw up, just like everyone else.

Accepting this fact and letting the user know when we make mistakes is the first step toward building trust. It helps diffuse the situation and shows that you can admit when you are wrong. When dealing with ISPs the users are often in a weak position simply because they know less about the subject. They already feel vulnerable and powerless in the face of their problem, they know less and they need the services to do their job. An ISP that talks and acts as if they can do no wrong certainly doesn't help users feel at ease. But a department that is transparent and admits when a mistake happens humanizes the interaction, and over time can make ISP the good guys.

But mistakes must be followed by corrective action to make it right, and screwing up cannot become a habit.

Action items
- Deliver good customer service
- Actively manage expectations
- Develop a process to manage complaints

Manage your clients

Managing clients

In step 1 we've seen how important it is to manage users through their lifecycle. In this section we will talk about the internal client: the decision-maker for a group of users. Internal clients could be a vice president, a director or a team leader for a department or team. The client is the person responsible for managing resources to achieve the objectives for the group.

A lot of internal service suppliers react negatively when I talk about managing their internal clients. It sounds a little bit like marketing. They feel their role as an internal service provider is to serve, not "manage" clients. It may sound a little too Machiavellian for them.

But the reality is that "managing" isn't a bad word. In fact, clients welcome it. Clients want their supplier to take an active interest in what they do, to adapt services to their needs, and to tell clients when they have unreasonable expectations. Your clients have the same issues you do, they need to get more done with less, and they need to know what you can and cannot do for them.

Let's look at two mechanisms you can use to manage clients: the account plan and the account review.

Managing a relationship through an account plan

Account plans have been in use for years by sales organizations to help them manage their work and prioritize resources. As much as sales organization would like to be helping all of their clients, the reality is that not all clients represent a real opportunity, and spending time and effort on them is a waste. On the other hand, key accounts must be nurtured and appropriately planned for to make sure that every interaction with them help drive the objectives forward, whether you're making a sale, securing a renewal or making sure the client is happy with the service they are getting.

How does this relate to internal service providers? An account plan can help internal service providers define a relationship with a client, set objectives to move the account forward and prioritize resources to meet the client's needs.

What's in an account plan?

An account plan is an internal document that is used by the team to help assess the needs of your clients, assess the health of your relationship, and define objectives and action items for the future. It helps identify and prioritize the activities required to build a strong, lasting relationship. It is not meant to be shared with the client; that is what the account review is for.

A good account plan can change the relationship with a client from reactive to systematic. By creating clear goals and objectives for each account, you can better manage the relationship with clients.

A typical account plan has five major components:
1. Account overview
2. Relationship assessment
3. Solution strategy
4. Delivery strategy
5. Action plan.

1. Account Overview:

Gives a sense of the size and complexity of the account. Identifies the major stakeholders.

The Account Overview is a description of the client department or team and lists the factors that influence service delivery. The overview provides information about the client, like size, complexity, if an ISP employee is assigned to the account, potential roadblocks. For example, if you work in HR your account overview will include the number and type of employees, their levels (professionals, unionized, etc.) as well as their complexity (highly educated vs. manual labourer). This information can also be compared to the rest of the organization to give a sense of how the group differs from others.

2. Solution Strategy:
The applications / services used by the client. Can be mapped to industry solutions (if one exists)

The Solution Strategy includes the solutions that are provided to the clients from your ISP. For example, in IT, solutions would represent the different tools and applications that are available to the client. In HR, solutions would represent the different services offered (payroll, recruitment, benefits, etc.). This list should include the scope of solutions that are delivered to the department, and would compare it to the rest of the organization.

The Solution Strategy should also compare those solutions to the rest of the industry to help identify potential gaps and future needs. For instance, a sales organization that doesn't use a customer relationship management application will likely want one very soon. This comparison is helpful in determining the client's focus areas in upcoming years.

3. Delivery Strategy:
The services used by the client and the client's satisfaction with them

The Delivery Strategy represents the mechanisms your client uses to interact with your internal service department. It covers the different channels used (phone, email, in-person) as well as the methods that facilitate the use of your solutions (support, project management, training). The satisfaction of the users is determined for each of these services, either by estimating it or by measurement. Whenever possible, the satisfaction should be compared to the whole of the organization, as well as individual departments.

These comparisons help define the differences between service delivery and client's expectations. If your help-desk consistently rates lower in its interactions with sales than with other departments, you know that either you are not providing what sales needs (salespeople are typically mobile for example) or that sales' expectations are too high, or sometimes both. Understanding these differences can help initiate the right conversations and adapt your service delivery to better serve your clients' needs.

4. Relationship Assessment:
The actual and desired personality profile and the health of the relationship between the ISPs and its clients.

As mentioned before, the personality profile desired by the business can actually vary from one internal client to another. But by understanding their expectations, you can start adapting your own personalities and services to meet their desires. Alternatively, you can start managing their expectations to make them more realistic with the rest of the organization.

An assessment of the health of the relationship can also help uncover lingering issues, personality conflicts or other obstacles that could stand in the way of building a strong partnership. Understanding that a key client stakeholder has a major conflict with one of your key personnel can explain a lot of the behaviours you see from both sides. Understanding the working relationship health is the first step in bridging the gap between expectations and what is delivered.

5. Action Plan:
The specific objectives, strategies and activities the ISP uses to service the client

The Action Plan is a list of the objectives for the next 3, 12 and 36 months with this account. How do you want the relationship with this account to evolve? How are you going to adapt or evolve your solutions to better meet their needs, modify your services to improve satisfaction, and remove solutions no longer working or required? These are not easy answers. You won't get all the answers correct on the first attempt, but the Action Plan will help you to start taking a critical look at the account on a regular basis. It isn't rare for an ISP to begin with only a 3-month plan, and then building the rest of the plan as they learn more about the needs of their clients.

That sounds like a lot of work
It is a lot of work, but typically not for the reason you think. Account plans are fairly small documents, typically 5-6 pages in PowerPoint that takes only minutes to complete. Our website includes templates that can guide you with both format and content.

The hardest part is the personal reflection that is required to assess the health of the relationship, define objectives and identifies strategies and action plans to help move the relationship, the client and your department or team forward. It requires understanding the realities of your front-line people's skills, understanding the needs of your clients and putting it together in a plan that makes sense. The good news is that this is an-ever evolving process. The account plan should be updated quarterly, which gives you ample opportunity to continually refine things as times goes by.

Improving communications through account reviews

The account review process provides a periodic (typically quarterly) check-in with the client to review the status of the service and help gauge the health of the relationship. This type of review has been shown to greatly improve relationships.

The account review is a chance for the internal service provider to showcase its performance to its clients. As we've seen clients spend very little time thinking about you, and when they do it's typically because something is going wrong. Having a formal review forces the client to think of your services in more rational terms, to see what is working and what is not, and understand the actions you are putting in place to stay or become a good service provider.

The account review is also an opportunity for the client to assess the services received and provide guidance and direction to you for the future. It gives clients an opportunity to voice their opinion on each of the solutions and services delivered, to discuss present and future needs and prioritize the order those needs should be addressed. It gives them an opportunity to discuss the entire breadth of the ISP's solutions and services, instead of simply looking at issues and problems. It also provides an opportunity to guide the evolution of the common tools that are shared by everyone within the organization.

But most importantly, it keeps communication open. Too often, internal service providers have very little communication with their clients, preferring the "no news is good news" approach. But no news isn't good news, and having a formal discussion every quarter promotes better relationships and results in clients becoming more inclined to reach out when something isn't right or when they feel their ISP should be part of an important conversation. It helps build partnerships.

How to conduct an account review

The account review is a quarterly (typically) meeting scheduled with each of the internal clients individually. The meeting is facilitated by a document that contains six major parts:

1. Operational performance
2. Service usage
3. Focus and priorities
4. On-going / new projects
5. Status and issues
6. Upcoming events

1. Operational performance:

The performance of the internal service provider in providing services.

We have already discussed the importance of measuring service delivery. This is the chance to show how good (or bad) the services were provided in the last quarter. This helps the client reset their perception of your actual performance instead of relying on water-cooler comments. It is also an opportunity to demonstrate your integrity by talking about performance problems, but also talk about the actions you've taken to correct incorrect situations.

2. Service usage:

How the client uses the services provided as compared to other clients. Opportunities for improving service usage.

Clients also want to know if their employees are using your services properly. By showing comparisons with other departments (when appropriate) you can demonstrate how well the client's employees are using the services. For example, a department that makes twice as many calls to the help-desk might be suffering from less reliable solutions, but could also simply be less knowledgeable, and perhaps some training would make a difference in reducing those calls.

3. Focus and priorities:

The clients' projects that will be a priority for the next quarter.

What are the priorities of the client? Is a major event coming up? This will allow you to understand the priorities of the client in their own terms. This information allows you to align you own priorities with what the clients are doing, so that you can fully support them. It also helps prevent surprises, ensuring that you are involved at the right time if a major initiative or event arises.

4. On-going / new projects
The on-going / new projects and major milestones that are being worked on.

This section describes the status of each major initiative (typically with a red, yellow, green code) that impacts the client. It provides a quick update of the health and key dates of the project. Each project will typically have its own status report, but chances are the client never gets a chance to look at them all at once and evaluate their impact. Two projects will be completed at the same time? Perhaps that is too much for the users to absorb at one time. It is easier to change plans earlier rather than later.

5. Status and issues:
On-going issues and their status from the last account review.

Chances are several issues will be uncovered in the account review meeting. Issues also arise between meetings, from the client itself or from its employees. This section lists all of the issues that were identified from the last account review as well as their status. This shows the client that you take all issues seriously until resolved and gives a sense of progress to the client that things are improving.

6. Upcoming events:
A summary of events that will impact the client.

This final section lists all of the events that might have an impact on the client. This list gives an opportunity for the client to identify any potential conflicts with what you are doing. A major software upgrade happening during an important event? Wouldn't it be easier to accomplish with three months warning than the week before? Employee performance evaluations are due at the same time as quarter end? Perhaps that deadline can be extended right away. This form of planning helps prevent issues in the long-term.

But I already talk to my clients

When I talk about formalizing the account review process with my clients, the first reaction I typically get is "But I already talk to my clients frequently, I don't need a formal meeting." Good. It's important to have a strong channel of communication open with your clients. You want them to feel comfortable calling you anytime they have an issue, a question or an idea.

But the overall intent of the meeting is to be intentional in your relationship. Chances are you do not take the opportunity to review operational performance, service usage, areas of priorities, projects, issues and upcoming events systematically in your on-going conversations. Typically, these informal conversations focus on a specific issue or project. By having a formal time set every quarter to review these topics you make sure that it gets done. It also shows your clients that you take these things very seriously and that you value their feedback.

See some examples of account plans and account reviews

You can visit the resource page on our web site: www.GreenElephantTeam.com/research to find templates, checklists and examples of account plans and account reviews.

Action items
- Develop an account plan for each major internal client
- Hold account review with your internal clients

Plan ahead

Become boringly predictable

My wife is a very predictable partner in our day-to-day lives. She works at my daughter's school, where the schedule is fixed, and enforced by bells throughout the day, and I can be sure she will always be home by 4:15. My wife is boringly predictable and it is a good thing. I don't have to worry about who will pick up my daughter after school, or the timing of the pickup.

On the other hand, I have the potential to be a very unreliable partner. Some weeks I work out of my home office every day, doing research and writing, while other weeks I will be juggling conferences, client meetings and workshops in different cities. My schedule is far from being boringly predictable. How do I make up for that? By planning carefully.

The goal of a partnership is not for it to be exciting. Rather, good partners tend to be boringly predictable. Partners are systematic in the ways they do things that involve each other, in how they react and avoid surprises at all costs by looking ahead. In this section we will see how you can become boringly predictable yourself. Don't worry, it's a good thing.

Building trust

We all have that friend whom we love tremendously but wouldn't leave alone in our house for the week-end. Not that they are malicious, but you just cannot trust them. They might break something, throw a party, harass the neighbours, lose the cat. You've never actually seen this friend behave this way, but you've heard stories. Entertaining stories perhaps, but the kind that have a very negative impact on his reputation, and makes you want to avoid him.

There are two major components that affect trust: your reputation and communication.

We already talked about the need to communicate with your internal clients. Effective communication helps develop a working relationship and eliminates misunderstandings that can cause issues. But reputation precedes all of this and will dictate if your internal clients will give you a chance or not.

I once knew a very solid manager, someone that worked hard, didn't count his hours and was always there when needed. He would always act with integrity and honesty. He was clearly an example of courage and dedication. But he was utterly disorganized. Nothing that impacted his performance, only simple things. He would show up late to meetings, but only by a few minutes. He would forget to send a meeting agenda for meetings he called, so people didn't really know the meeting subject. Once the meeting was over it was never entirely clear what had to be done, and he would often forget to send meeting minutes or a summary.

The net result: this person's reputation was shot. He stagnated in his position and most people avoided having to work with him. And even though he was funny and sympathetic, no one would leave him the key to their house.

Reputation is based on your day-to-day decisions and behaviours. Every time you act with integrity the reputation improves a little bit. Every time you stand up for your clients' your reputation gets better. But every time you act the other way, your reputation drops dramatically.

Easy ways to lose trust

Trust is hard to earn, but very easy to lose. And the unfortunate part is that you might not realize that your client is losing trust in you, until it is too late. Few people will directly tell you that you are becoming untrustworthy. But the signs might be there; perhaps they are avoiding talking to you.

There are four ways internal service providers lose the trust of their clients:

- Skills and competencies: Lacks the ability to deliver work through either a lack of skills, a lack of problem solving or by being inconsistent or sloppy in their work.
- Interpersonal relationships: Not listening to clients, being insensitive to their concerns or failing to ask for their input.
- Integrity: Internal service providers that violate the confidence of their clients, by lying or talking about the client behind their back.
- Dependability: Fail to do what they committed to, being disorganized or not following up.

Looking at this list, you could say, "All you have to do is be professional".

Mind the small things

An easy way to lose trust is by being careless in our day-to-day activities. For example, most executives spend roughly a third of their time in meetings. But, how many meetings have you been in recently that have started on time? A large percentage of meetings start late, with people showing up as much as 5 to 10 minutes after the start. And many organizational cultures still tolerate this.

Late meetings are also a good way to appear unprofessional and disorganized. How can I trust you to deliver an important project if you can't even be on-time for a meeting? Think about your own providers and the kind of impression they leave when they are late. The fact that you are in the same family, company or department doesn't change the client-supplier dynamic.

Although these matters can appear simplistic, they are key components of a trusting relationship.

Do you know what you'll do next year?
I've been helping internal service providers become better partners for years. And most internal service providers are very passionate at becoming a strategic partner to their clients. They want to bring value to the business by helping clients with their strategic planning activities, defining orientations that will impact the organization for years to come. They genuinely care about helping the company move forward and become more competitive and productive. I've heard many times "If only the business had a plan, we could align to it and help to reach their objectives for the company. " And of course they would be more than willing to help the business draft such a plan.

Bu then we stop daydreaming, and I start asking some questions: can I see your internal service provider strategic plan? No, we don't have one. Can I see a list of the projects you have underway at present? We might have one but it is probably not up to date. Ok, perhaps an organizational chart? Again, we have one but it's probably out of date.

The reality is that most internal service providers suffer from the same problems their clients do: lack of forward planning. Everyone is so caught up in their day-to-day that no one has time to sit down and think about the activities they will have to do in the future.

Lead by example
Would you take financial advice from someone who is broke? Or

diet advice from someone who is overweight? It is pretty difficult to understand an internal service provider that volunteers to help with our strategic plan when they don't have one themselves. And nothing kills predictability more than announcing to a company that we need to do major maintenance immediately because our suppliers are forcing us to change software version. All of these activities can be planned months, if not years, in advance.

A quarter at a time
Most people think that planning involves a high degree of certainty, that every project and initiative must be precise to the day, if not the hour. Planning software (like MS project) leaves many professionals uneasy as it imposes a precision that most people are not comfortable with.

What you do need though, is some idea of the projects that will be tackled when. And as the time horizon comes closer, then precision about the project and time should increase.

I typically recommend the following type of planning for my clients:

- Current quarter: Precise to a couple of days
- Next quarter: Precise to a week
- Next year: Precise to a month
- Next 2 years: Precise to a quarter

But keep in mind that these types of timelines are only for dates that impact a client. Not everything needs to be planned to a couple of days. But if you plan on shutting systems down, or delivering a major piece of work, then you should aim to respect your stated due dates.

But your plans should be flexible. Does a new event or issue impact your planning? Change the plan. That's the whole point of planning, to allocate resources and anticipate problems. No one expects that a plan will never change.

Communicate the plan

The most important part of any plan: communication. A plan that sits on your desk or hard drive is useless to everyone. Your plan should be communicated to your internal clients, partners, suppliers and, of course, your own team.

Your plan should also be a tool that you use in your daily activities. If you are running a team or department meeting without your plan in hand then you are planning to fail.

Are you on the list?

Internal service providers typically receive a deluge of requests every day. Clients want changes to computer systems, they want to modify a HR policy, or they want new templates for supplier contracts. Requests abound, unfortunately internal service providers cannot address them all. Demand exceeds supply dramatically.

So what typically ends up happening? We make a list of all the requests, projects, initiatives, etc. Some people keep the list open all the time, so users can add new initiatives any time. Others have date-driven intake periods, give time windows when users and clients can submit requests, with a date after which no more requests will be taken.

Some companies will go to great lengths to properly prioritize the items on the list. They will setup processes to evaluate requests, compare their benefits against the objectives of the organization and ask a cross-departmental steering committee to help approve and prioritize the items. Unfortunately, this process typically only occurs a year at a time, leaving everything else in a constant state of uncertainty. Will it get done next year? We don't know. It depends if it makes the cut when next year's requests are evaluated.

Managing expectations around the list

Internal service providers typically don't like saying no to their clients. They would rather keep project on the list indefinitely than let a client know it will probably not happen. They see this as a nice way to avoid a difficult conversation, and they don't ever have to actually say no to the client.

But clients would rather hear the real story. If something will take two years to get done, or won't be done at all, then they can make other arrangements. You can't make the requested change to the system? Then we'll develop a procedure to facilitate things in another way. By saying no you at least give them an opportunity to fix the problem on their own instead of waiting for a solution that never comes.

And going back to our principle of predictability, saying no helps the internal service provider be more transparent and predictable, which in turn increases trust.

Rolling plan of initiative

Internal service providers can address the situation by developing a rolling plan of initiatives and requests. By comparing the amount of work and current capacity, ISP can identify the expected quarter that each request can be completed. And by reviewing the plan continuously (typically once a quarter), new initiatives can be added and the entire list reprioritized.

What's the difference with the previous method? Now clients have an expected delivery date. If they are not happy with the date, they can do something about it. If their priority is too far in the future, they can at least know it will most likely never get done and act accordingly.

Action items
•   Don't lose trust by being unprofessional

- Develop a one to three year plan of activities
- Plan projects over a three year period

Summary - Value Plan

1. Deliver the basics	2. Manage alignment	3. Demonstrate value
• Measure • Manage the life-cycle • Understand the users	• Team alignment • Vision alignment • Business alignment	• Manage satisfaction • Manage your clients • Plan ahead

Removing obstacles

But, it won't work at my company
If you've read this book thus far, it probably means that you pretty much agree with what we're saying. Perhaps you already started drafting your Value Plan of Attack, identifying ways you can better deliver the Basics and maybe you even already know what the business expects in term of personality profile.

But there is also a chance that you are thinking: "That's all nice and good, but it won't work in my organization". Your organization is different. These concepts are great for others, but your organization makes applying these principles difficult, or even impossible.

I disagree.

We will look at the three major obstacles to deliver value: lack of time, lack of resources and finally lack of interest and some strategies to address them.

Organize yourself or you'll get organized

When I was young, my dad use to say "Organize yourself or you'll get organized!". That typically meant that I had to do whatever he was asking at the time, and that if I didn't organize my time properly, he would do it for me (with more chores typically). Although it would infuriate me at the time, it still resonate today. People that can't organize themselves often end up getting organized by others, but not always in a way they like.

Your days are very busy, you run around from one meeting to another, barely finding time to have lunch. How are you going to find time to focus on user service if you are barely keeping up with all the fires happening during the day?

A research conducted by the Family and Work Institute showed that fifty-four percent of American employees have felt overwhelmed at some time in the past month by how much work they had to complete.

So you are not alone. But what differentiates professionals that successfully manage their time from the others?

Make the time

They make the time for it. You will always have more things to do than you can really tackle. But by prioritizing value creation they build an environment where they are able to dictate their priorities. Successful managers start their day thinking about their service and their objectives. Reactive managers start their day checking their emails.

Emails are terrible way to manage work. First, they are focused on people asking you for things. Second, new emails keep popping up, distracting you from the task at hand. Successful time managers disable the notifications from their emails (yes, including the phone) and check their emails whenever it is convenient for them (typically 3-4 times a day) instead of when it is convenient for the sender.

Successful leaders are very protective of their time. Does this meeting need to be done in one hour or would 30 minutes be enough? Is the prep work and meeting agenda done before the meeting? Are people on time? Can I delegate this meeting to someone else?

Avoid procrastination through crisis

Second, they get comfortable living close to fires. There will always be the "crisis of the day", something is not working, a high-level executive is asking for a special report, a key supplier hasn't shown up. And it would be easy for a manager to spend all of its time going from one crisis to another, solving problems and guiding people with its amazing leadership skills.

Fighting crisis as an extreme form of procrastination. You know you have some hard, demanding tasks ahead of you, but crisis are right there to be addressed, waiting to take your mind off these difficult problems. And crisis gives an instant reward, compared to these other boring tasks that will only show benefits in weeks, if not months from now.

Not every crisis need to be addressed right away and by you. Sometimes, it's ok to simply give others your general guidelines and ask them to keep you in the loop.

Only big companies can afford this kind of service

Big internal service departments have understood that they need to invest in their user service capabilities. Most have already invested in systems to track user requests (through support tickets for example) so that no requests falls between the tracks. They invest in project management systems to help them plan their work and anticipates resource conflicts. They even have specific roles (such as the business relationship manager) to help them manage the relationship with the business. Resources and economies of scales justifies such investments.

But what about small departments?

What if you are a team of one? Back when I was CIO I had the marketing department reporting to me. Now, marketing for an industrial manufacturing is pretty limited, the entire department consisted of one graphic designer whose name was Mark. The different sales group would reach out to him to design new collateral, ads and promotional products. But the fact that he was alone wasn't an obstacle for him to act as a real internal service provider.

Mark kept an annual planning calendar that listed everything that needed to be done. Yellow Pages renewal, past years promotional campaigns, web ads, and even internal communications. Mark was frequently seen reaching out to his internal clients to remind them a new campaign was probably due. He would analyze the effectiveness of the different ads and make recommendations to his partners. He would even make experiments on the website, comparing the results of different approaches or messages.

Mark was a true Agent.

Big or small: it's all the same

Whether you are a team of one, a leader of a small, efficient team or part of huge departments, the same principles applies. The difference will be in the level of sophistication of the tools and processes that will support the service delivery. A huge department can afford to put in place a system to handle user request while a team of one might be productive just using his email system. Big departments need detailed processes to handle work and keep the wheels aligned while a small team might be efficient just by communicating and working tightly.

But regardless of size, budget and type of organization, providing value is matter of daily attitude and behaviour. It isn't easier for big departments with lots of tools. At the end of the day, it's the attitude that counts.

My boss doesn't care!

Here's a pretty typical story. Bob, a HR leader wants to take a greater role within its company. He thinks he can really provide value to the business units, after all he know the company pretty well, understands the industry and has some good ideas on how to make the processes between business units easier. He really sees himself with the potential of becoming an Agent, someone that can help drive the organization to greater productivity and performance.

He goes to his boss with a few of his ideas to improve his own service and to improve the business. And that's when his bubble bursts. In no uncertain terms, the boss tells him that his role is not to become a great service provider, and certainly not to tell the business how it should run. His job is to hire people when needed, pay them and make sure the company doesn't get sued. If he has time to do anything else, then it means he has too many people working for him.

Congratulations! You've just identified one of the expectations from the business. Your boss is looking for an Accountant, someone that can deliver basic services at a low price. They don't want someone to deliver over the top service, or someone that generate ideas and contribute to the direction of the business. They want a solid, cost-effective providers. And there is nothing wrong with that.

If you remember, we talked about the potential issues vision alignment could have on an internal service provider. In this case, your group is clearly not aligned with your boss' vision (Agent VS Accountant), which can lead to severe misunderstandings and frustrations.

Should I stay or should I go?

Do you want to be an Accountant? In the case of Bob, chances are no. Someone that is naturally inclined to learn about the business and try to generate improvement ideas will be miserable in the role of an Accountant. Being an Accountant requires a constant obsession with numbers, pouring over spreadsheets and contracts to find opportunities to reduce costs. It also requires a certain immunity to user complaints, being able to brush off negative comments for the sake of keeping operations efficient.

Bob has an important choice to make
1. Stay in his miserable job, and slowly see his initiative drain away
2. Leave, realizing that this work environment won't allow him to play to his strengths
3. Change his boss' expectations.

Your boss doesn't believe you can add value

The problem comes form the experiences, beliefs and biases associated with you or your department. Perhaps Bob's boss doesn't believe HR can play a strategic role. Perhaps he just doesn't see Bob's potential. At the end of the day, the Boss doesn't see the value. Sound familiar?

By following the steps in the Value Plan (1. Deliver the Basics, 2. Manage alignment and 3. Demonstrate value), you can change the expectations of your boss and even from the business units. Ideas are a dime a dozen, but when people start seeing concrete results, help and support typically starts to pour in.

I confess: I'm a Nanny

When I talk with new clients, one of the questions I like to ask is, "What do you think your personality profile is?" Of course, most people answer that they are Agents. Being an Agent seems to be the best of both worlds: a high service orientation to satisfy the users, combined with a high business orientation to influence the organization. Of course, after we complete the assessment I find most of those who want to be Agents aren't. People would like to think they are Agents, but in reality they don't act like Agents in their day-to-day activities.

I'm the same; I'd like to think I'm an Agent. But I admit it, I'm a Nanny. A pretty polarized one at that. Although I would love to say that I have a very high service orientation, in reality I'm much more preoccupied with meeting objectives, whatever it takes.

In this section we'll look at my experiences as a Nanny working as a CIO. I was fortunate to work in a great organization, with a very talented team and solid executives. There was plenty of money and a strong commitment to meet objectives. All of the ingredients were in place for a successful project, yet we'll see that even in the best of cases, things are never easy.

The context

I had been working as consultant for Gartner, a renowned IT management consulting firm for almost ten years when a new client asked me to evaluate if his company was ready to implement a major business transformation project. The company had gone through a series of acquisitions in different regions and countries, and was all over the place in terms of its processes and systems.

The client was in the rendering industry, basically using leftover parts of animals after the slaughterhouse, grinding it up, cooking it and reselling the result as pet food. Huge 18-wheelers of animal carcasses were rolled into the plant every day and the contents dumped into enormous pits. The sight and smell of the operation was quite powerful, for some people it was overwhelming. So overwhelming that the company had stopped training new hires, preferring to let them do menial tasks in the plant for a couple of weeks, to see if they would be able to stand the environment. It made no sense to train people who would quit because they couldn't put up with the smell.

Call me morbid, but something in this company fascinated me. Prior to this I had always worked with insurance, IT or some other white-collar company and had never been inside an operation like a rendering plant before. So when I was given the opportunity to take on this project I agreed, on the condition that I could visit the plants, which they were more than happy to oblige.

After doing an initial readiness assessment, I came to a strange conclusion: they were not ready to tackle this project, but they should go forward with the project anyway. For the past two years, the company had tried to map and reengineer its business processes without success. Talented consultants were brought in to facilitate workshops, but what was produced was unusable. The different departments of the business, and its facilities in different locations, saw the world very differently. It would be impossible for the company to realize economies of scale until they could all agree on a common way of doing things.

The strategy I proposed was to create a sense of urgency, a burning platform if you will, by setting an aggressive date and letting everyone know that the systems would be switched over by then, ready or not. This sense of urgency would help people be more reasonable in their requests and more conciliatory in designing new processes. Or so the theory went. I knew there would be consequences related to this approach, and I informed the client that they would probably experience a 5% to 10% employee turnover rate because some wouldn't be able to keep up and others would simply not want to work in such a tightly-regimented environment. That would be the cost of achieving the desired results. To my surprise, the owners accepted the approach.

But to do such a project they would need a different type of leader. They were used to managing by consensus, but to have success they would need someone more dictatorial, who could drive the initiative forward, regardless of the consequences. Someone organized and highly talented who could push the project forward whatever it took. In a nutshell: a Nanny.

Getting in

The CFO was a very sharp, energetic executive who had been in various companies and implemented many reengineering projects. Having experience in this area, he was very conscious of the price the organization would pay to achieve something of this magnitude. He hired a recruitment firm to find someone to lead this initiative, but no one seemed to fit the profile. As I reviewed my own list of clients with him, trying to find a CIO that would be interested in such a project, he came to a conclusion: I should be the one leading the project.

For the previous ten years I had been a consultant, giving IT management advice and letting the clients handle the execution. But a part of me had always wondered if I could handle being on the other side of the fence, being accountable for results, instead of just giving advice. Could I live with the daily rigor of operations, helping an entire company change while simultaneously delivering a major project? It was a challenge that was hard to refuse. Helping my decision were the facts that my daughter was about to start school, getting off the road would be great, and being able to settle somewhere sounded appealing. I said yes.

As soon as I said yes, I knew I was in for a strange ride. The CFO informed me that despite offering me the job, he still had to follow HR's process which included an interview by the employees who would report to me. Now my agenda was pretty clear. I knew I would have to let a large portion of these people go since their skill sets were not right for this project. And now they would interview me? This is on my top 5 most surreal and awkward situations I have faced in my life. But I still got the job.

Starting up

The project started with a bang. The project manager assigned to the initiative left. That wasn't a big deal since my plan was to replace him anyway, but he left earlier than I had planned for. No worries, I had someone else in mind. When I asked him to come earlier than discussed, he informed me he wouldn't be able to take the job, because a previous commitment with a client had come up and he couldn't leave them in trouble. That conscientiousness is one reason I wanted to hire him, so what could I say? So... I had a new job, a project fixed start date and a fixed end date 9 months later. And I had no project manager.

Any sane person would have revisited the date and postponed the project for a while. I mean, how could we start a project without a project manager or a project team and without a signed contract with a supplier? But I decided to keep the dates. The CFO (my boss) thought I was crazy. But I must have been pretty convincing since he went along with my plan.

Working with some very talented external partners, I recruited a project manager and some key people, and we signed a contract with a supplier and assembled a project team. Doing all this in such a short amount of time required a lot of creativity, aggressiveness and mostly, corner cutting. All the corner cutting didn't win me any friends in the organization. I had by-passed most of HR's rules for recruiting, going to a recruiting firm directly, conducting employment interviews myself (without HR) and promising jobs even if the paperwork (and HR's due diligence) wasn't complete. And I was signing contracts left and right without their legal and finance involvement. Not a good way to start a harmonious relationship.

The other departments understood the urgency of the situation, and while they may not have liked the approach, they were very cooperative and helpful. They agreed to the accelerated process and patched the holes I created in my mad quest to start the project.

1. Building credibility
The users
Users had been neglected for some time. In fact, that's not entirely true. The users working in the three administrative offices were served very well. However, the employees at the 22 plants were woefully neglected. The plants typically ran 24 hours a day, 6 days a week. The seventh day was used for maintenance and repairs. Yet, IT support was available only during regular business hours. And it really wasn't "support." Officially, the only way to receive support was to email your request, even if your problem was that your email didn't work. Alternatively, you could hunt down one of the tech support guys if you could find one and beg him to come work on your problem right away. Of course, that option was only available to users at headquarters since IT staff was located there.

Even in the headquarters building the support varied based on how important you were. Administrative assistant to a VP? Then you would get instant support, even if they had to stop working with another user. If you were a clerk in HR then you'd better be patient. New equipment was also provided by this method, VIPs and friends being served first. As you could imagine this led to a lot of animosity since it was not only unfair, but also careless.

Outsourcing support

To improve the support process, I decided to outsource support completely. One advantage of outsourcing support was that it brought uniformity to the process. While VIPs had a reduction in service, plant employees got an immediate increase in service. Everyone was now getting the same level of support. Of course, everyone was not happy about it. Those users who used to be able to call Bob in IT and get help right away now had to work on the phone with a support specialist who asked a series of diagnostic questions. And there was no more favoritism with new equipment. Want a new mouse? You'll get whatever is the standard, not the cool one you saw at Best Buy.

But predictability does have its advantages. Users started to realize that they could get requests handled very quickly, that they could actually rely on the support team to get things done.

Measuring service

To quantify the credibility of the department, I began taking monthly user satisfaction surveys. Each month we asked 1/6th of the users what they thought of the services the received, so every user got surveyed twice a year. Participation was spotty at first, because users did not believe that the survey would change anything. But I followed up with every negative comment, thanking them for their time and explaining what would or would not be done. The word quickly spread within the organization that the survey was actually being read and concrete actions taken in response.

The results of the survey were communicated in the monthly IT department meeting. Variations in support levels were explained by the different service owners. This monthly reporting served as a constant reminder that satisfaction was important, as much as a budget or project. At first the reaction of the staff was to dismiss bad comments, saying things like, "Well these guys are never happy, nothing will change that!" But as time went by, people started to recognize that it was possible to change user perceptions.

I also communicated the survey results in the monthly executive committee meetings. At first, the other executives laughed, not believing the results I showed them. But every month I would show up with new numbers, good or bad, explain the variations and what I would do to correct it. Over time, the survey became a staple of the meeting. In fact, the president started turning to the other groups, asking them for their satisfaction scores. I didn't make any friends this way either.

Together with the monthly survey I also implemented a post-support survey, where one out of every eight support requests was followed with a quick satisfaction survey asking about their experience. The external supplier was responsible if satisfaction dropped and also had penalties for missing satisfaction targets. The targets and penalties ensure the supplier was focused on the right priorities and trying to close calls as quickly as possible.

Internally, the measurement program was a tough sell. The staff had never been held accountable and felt that it wasn't fair to hold them responsible for satisfaction since many elements were outside of their control. Over time they began seeing the factors contributing to satisfaction, and were able to influence the satisfaction levels with their expertise. They also realized that technical skills alone wouldn't be enough and started spending time learning more about customer service.

For me, this process was very taxing. As a typical Nanny, I like putting in place new processes and methodologies, but rating satisfaction day after day required a level of commitment I hadn't anticipated. Following up with the dissatisfied users was also interesting. Hearing complaints and how service failed them in a time of need is never fun. But their complaints provided valuable feedback that helped me make the right decisions over time.

Understanding the users

I was new to the industry, and it showed. I regularly used wrong terminology, didn't understand some discussions when they became too specific and didn't realize the magnitude of the company's operations. I decided to remedy this by setting myself a very big objective: I would know more about the company than any other executive. That probably sounds arrogant to think I could know more than people who have worked there for more than twenty years, but few people really understand everything that happens in a company from A to Z. They typically understand a smaller part like a department or a specific role, but rarely the entire process. And much of what people do understand is typically obsolete, dating back from the time they were on the ground floor themselves, which may have been many years ago.

I decided to tackle this challenge by systematically shadowing all of the major positions in the company and following the production process from A to Z. Keep in mind that the company recycled animal carcasses, so spending time at the plants and on the road wasn't the most appealing proposition. To make sure I wouldn't be the only one having fun, I shared the pleasure with my team members. Everyone got a brand new pair of steel-toed boots and a helmet and we went to work. We spent time looking over everyone's shoulder. Watching what they did, and asking questions one after the other. We did some of the work whenever we could (some work required specialized training or certifications). I even visited the slaughterhouses that provided the carcasses and the animal feed company that bought our product. I wanted to understand the process from beginning to end.

By the end of this learning process we were able to understand fully how the company operates, and correct some false beliefs held by the executive team. You thought that clients didn't want deliveries during lunch hour? Actually it's because the drivers like to meet up at a local strip joint for lunch. Wonder why plants are sometimes idle for long periods? It's because the transport team doesn't tell the plant when shipments are delayed. All of these little inconsistencies came to light, and long-held beliefs got challenged.

It also gave me the opportunity to better understand the reality of our users. Some drivers could barely read, and expecting them to use handheld computers was too much to ask from them. Some users had to work in five different applications simultaneously on one tiny screen, constantly switching back and forth. Learning these things allowed us to revisit our standard configurations to make users more effective (including providing several screens to customer service people).

Our presence at the plants and other activities helped improve our credibility in the field. Users saw that we were taking the time to understand what they did instead of relying on assumptions. They saw us walking around, asking questions, challenging. And they saw results from our visits. New equipment, new service hours, and services adapted to better meet their needs. In a matter of months we went from being the laughing stock of the organization to a decent service provider. In fact we were quickly replaced as the subject of cruel jokes by one of the other internal service providers. While taxing, these efforts helped to make the project a success later on.

2. Alignment
Aligning the team and the vision

As mentioned, the company had grown through acquisitions. That meant the IT team had bccomc a combination of IT groups based in different places. The relationship between these teams was so bad that they had agreed to not talk to each other. Instead, each group managed their own infrastructure and applications. I was trying to herd a team of French Canadians who hated their English Canadian colleagues, and an American team that refused to take orders from anyone north of the border.

So we had three separate infrastructures along with three set of applications, standards and tools. A user in the U.S. got completely different service than a user in Canada. Systems didn't talk to one another and it was very difficult to close the books at months end. Finance spent a large portion of their time trying to fix issues.

The teams also couldn't agree on their role. Some thought they were supposed to keep costs as low as possible (Accountant) and all of their decisions along this orientation, while others thought they should give everything the user asked for(Butler), after all, they were paying for it. The result is that some offices had state of the art equipment while others were getting by with yesterday's junk.

How does a Nanny react to this? Starting from scratch.

Instead of trying to rebuild the team and spend months, if not years, putting in place processes, redefining roles and mending relationships, I decided to outsource almost everything. Within the first couple of months I downsized the team by almost half. I contracted two different companies to take over the network and computing infrastructure. The servers that had been housed in actual closets were all moved to a secure facility with round-the-clock protection and support. The IT support team was outsourced to an offshore company that provided 24/7 support (to match the plants schedules) instead of the 9-5 that was provided previously. I kept in-house the project people and a few promising technicians.

I also hired quite a few new people, talented individuals from other industries and companies who brought in a more robust set of skills and management practices than what was currently in place.

In a matter of months, the team was unrecognizable. This made the old team members, and the users they supported, very anxious. Not everyone agreed with the new orientations. Several doubted the soundness of outsourcing almost everything, basically giving over the keys to an outside partner. Several saw this as a major risk, and a slap in the face, like saying everything they had done for years was wrong.

My gut instinct was to brush their concerns aside. If they knew what they were doing then I wouldn't be there in the first place. But their concerns grew bigger, they became more vocal and they also began looking for conflict at meetings, at lunch, wherever they could find an audience. The relationship between the external vendors and the internal team quickly degenerated. Problems became impossible to resolve, each party blaming the other. Executives saw the dissent and started to question the orientation themselves. After all, what does it say when a leader's team doesn't agree with his decisions?

It took some time to resolve these issues. Some employees decided they couldn't work in the environment and left. Others decided to invest some time in understanding the vision and the constraints and they learned that going outside helped us gain instant maturity, something that would have been difficult to do internally given the circumstances. I did quite a bit of work to reassure people that I didn't think everything was wrong before, but instead that new initiatives demanded new orientations. I communicated the vision, later than I really should have, but the result was beneficial.

Business alignment

Shortly after the project started, the anvil fell: corporate restructuring. The company had too many vice-presidents and decided to streamline its structure, moving from a matrix structure to a leaner traditional one. In the process it replaced key leadership positions. Anyone doing a major project will tell you that one of the biggest risks is a change of corporate leadership. New leaders mean new approaches, visions and priorities. Most people would have put the project on hold until the new management team determined its orientation, and would have waited for the dust to settle before doing anything major. But that was other people. I decided to keep going, just like any other Nanny would.

The new management team came from a different company, one that was much more cost-conscious. In fact, the company was renowned for being extremely aggressive in cost management, astute in negotiations and good at squeezing suppliers. A very traditional manufacturing company, it had a culture of tight cost-controls. Of course, that meant that their internal service suppliers were more along the line of Accountants or Butlers than Nannies. The new team expected a totally different role for the CIO than the one I was playing, and they wondered why I was sitting at "adult" table.

This clash between the new team's expectation and my own personality profile was the root of many conflicts that would arise during my four years at the company.

Of course, a new executive team wants to change things. In fact, they have to. Each executive typically has a specific mandate, whether it is to improve quality, solve a problem, reduce costs, increase sales or all of the above. These executives will not let an on-going project slow their initiatives, just like I wouldn't let their initiatives slow me down. That is all nice and good for the executives, but employees become stuck in between the power plays.

So while we were implementing a major business transformation project, the different business units were also embarking on their own projects and initiatives. The company had never seen such a high level of activity. Employees were being pulled from all directions, being asked to participate in projects and initiatives while trying to keep company operations going. Stress and anxiety went through the roof. Users complained of burn-out. Employees regularly came in my office crying, telling me how their family situation was becoming difficult, how travel was causing problems, and in some cases how the stress was impacting their marriage. It was quickly becoming a crazy game of chicken and no one was willing to turn the steering wheel away.

So who won the game? Well, as you've probably guessed, the Nanny. There came a point when the owners had to step in and stop the madness. And since the business transformation project was one of the owners' pet projects, it got right-of-way while other projects got scaled back. A more rational approach might have been to reprioritize the projects together as a team, making decisions based on priorities and capacity. But no one was willing to sacrifice for the greater good, each thinking that their own initiative would bring the most benefits.

3. Demonstrate value
The project go-live date was quickly approaching and anxiety was starting to increase quite a bit. Executives were anxious, some asking for the project to be delayed. The organization was clearly not ready to embark on a change of this scale and frankly, neither was the project team. We still had major issues to resolve and deliverables that were running late. The level of risk was getting fairly high, and several members of the executive team thought we were heading toward a complete catastrophe if we kept going. I pushed to keep the date. My thinking was that if we start postponing now we will find a good reason to postpone again. So let's bite the bullet and get it done. But,

that is easy to say when you are implementing the change, not receiving it.

To make the project a success, I knew that some serious expectation management had to take place. Most users still thought they were getting a new computer system that looked like they had been using. They didn't realize the magnitude of change that was coming their way. They also didn't understand that the implementation would be accompanied by downsizing, the main driver for the project in the first place.

Change management

In order to identify the company's different needs, I chose to use an account planning approach with the different business units. We identified the services they used, how well they used them, their user satisfaction and how it compared with the rest of the company, and their areas that would be impacted by the new system. We sat down with each major leader to discuss these elements. We then developed an action plan to help them prepare. This exercise allowed us to prioritize activities within the business units, helping them realize what they had to do to prepare, and what we could do to help. These discussions were not always easy or even polite, but they did allow everyone to build relationships over time.

We worked with HR on the change management portion of the project, helping users understand how their lives would be impacted. I journeyed around giving roadshows, presenting the project and the new system, fielding concerns and answering questions with complete transparency. ("Will people lose their jobs?" "Yes, some of you will.") It was not fun. While I was doing this roadshow, I wanted to be back with the team to keep the project moving forward. A typical Nanny, I felt that driving the project was more important than managing user perceptions. Luckily, HR was very helpful at keeping me on track with these activities. Eventually we found out that what we did was still not sufficient, and that you can never invest too much time in change management.

One of my key preoccupations was setting the right expectations for the users. The project had been oversold in the organization, promising that work would be easier, systems faster and that reports would provide exactly what is needed when it is needed. It sold a future I couldn't possibly deliver. The roadshow, together with the team doing on-site demonstrations of the new system, helped reset expectations to a more realistic level. Users saw that it isn't an easy system, and that it would not do everything we wanted it to, because an easy, do everything system would just be too costly. Some transactions will be easier, but you won't see them since they will be automated. What you will see are the transactions that didn't work, the ones that will require you to dig deeper into the system to see what failed. It was a sobering experience for many, but users were thankful since it prepared them for the new systems go-live.

Communicating with the users

As we geared up, we established a fairly rigorous communication plan. We sent monthly project status communications to users, including short vignettes from the project team explaining the new processes. We made sure that the users knew the project team members, the suppliers' reps and the key users. We tried very hard to show the users that we were working for them.

In each of the communications I included my email and cell phone number, encouraging users to contact me. The communication team thought I was crazy, that I would get a deluge of complaints. But generally I only received a few calls every week, and most were very minor. Regardless of the importance, I made a point to follow up with each user. I would determine the status of the problem, call them and listen to their concerns. Some users would go on and on and really test my patience. Some made unrealistic requests and I explained to them that what they were asking for was impossible for me to deliver. But everyone saw that we took complaints seriously.

For the project to be a success, users would have to see value in it. Part of the project's intentions was to reduce costs (and it did), but it was also supposed to help users. To do so the system needed to make users' daily lives easier. We worked hard to remove unneeded things from the system. As we've seen, too many options can be bad for users. Having buttons, pages or screens that don't add value is a waste of time and adds confusion. The project team identified everything we could remove to make the users' lives easier. We also developed on-demand training resources. Since some activities are only done a few times a year by the users (expense accounts for example) and people forget them from one time to the next, we developed small videos that walked users through basic tasks. We did everything we could to make the system easy to use, to make the daily lives of our users better.

The result
We ended up delivering on time and on budget, which is rare for projects of this type. Of course it wasn't very smooth and the business worked very hard to correct any errors and then catch up on the backlog of regular work that the project's implementation created. In the end the project delivered as promised. In fact we received the Octas award for the enterprise application project of the year. The entire team was very excited and I was proud of them. Against all odds they had accomplished the seemingly impossible in a short amount of time.

Once the implementation was completed and the system and processes stabilized, the organization needed some rest. Everyone had worked tirelessly to make things work, to patch the parts that didn't work and to get everyone on-board with the new system. I was rewarded with more responsibilities, including being responsible for business processes and logistics which I knew nothing about. I was happy that I was on track to become an important player in the organization.

But the project wasn't entirely finished. In order to reap the next phase of benefits we would have to examine some fundamentals of the business, our interactions with clients and how our departments worked together. Unfortunately the appetite wasn't there anymore for another Big Bang project. The executive team opted for a softer approach, using some part-timers, to identify and implement opportunities throughout the organization.

I was against this approach. I also understood where they were coming from. We had spent so much time and energy working on one aspect of the company that we now needed some breathing room to get some other things done. The mission of the company isn't to transform itself, it is there to serve its clients and they had been neglected.

So I went along with the plan, which was a major mistake. Not because of the company or its approach, after all other companies take it slow and steady and it works for them. But it didn't work because of me.

Nannies are very focused. They like to get their projects going quickly and with intensity. Slow and steady just doesn't work for a Nanny. It was a situation where Agents would be in there element. An Agent could leverage the internal politics to get initiatives going. And an Agent would have been patient enough to let projects run their course. A Butler would also have been successful, working with the different business units to help them improve at their own pace. But this situation was not for a Nanny.

I became unfocused. I spread my resources over many initiatives, and had several smaller projects going at the same time to give the illusion of progress. My team felt my lack of focus and priority. Everyone was used to being super-committed, working hard and driving results. Now they had a hard time getting the different business units to cooperate. Meetings were cancelled and no one was following through on decisions. Morale started declining pretty rapidly and inter-departmental conflicts started to erupt.

I dreaded going to work. My days started feeling longer and longer, and I was looking forward to just heading home at night. Nannies don't do well in a pure operational management role. Without a big objective, it is difficult for Nannies to find the motivation to do the same things day after day.

This is perhaps one of the most important aspects of looking at personality profiles: alignment drives satisfaction. Accountants like looking at costs, Butlers like to serve, Agents like to play an important role, and Nannies like to be constantly focused.

Understanding your personality profile will allow you to find a role in which you can succeed, a role where you will be excited and motivated and feel like you are making a genuine contribution. That's true whether you manage an internal service provider, work as part of a team or are on the front-line supporting users. Alignment is the key.

CONCLUSION

Before you start you Value Journey

By applying the ISP personality profiles, and by following the Value Plan, an internal service provider can consistently engage its users and demonstrate its value. But before any of this partnership can happen, the ISP must first develop a culture of service within its own organization. For some groups, this require a significant shift. If the purpose of internal service providers is to service its internal clients, then it must first learn how to serve itself, learning to collaborate and help each other, so it can become a credible partner.

You can learn more on how internal service providers can demonstrate their value through satisfaction and partnership by visiting our web site www.GreenElephantTeam.com. You'll find research papers, presentations and webinars that explain each of these concepts in more details.

Appendix

An apology

I would like to apologize if I offended you by the terms I used. After all not all accountants are like my version of the Accountant and not all nannies are directive. They were meant to help readers quickly get a feel of the personality.

These names have proven to be quite effective within my clients, often becoming part of the internal vocabulary. I've heard people say things like "Stop acting like a Nanny, our users are not dumb!" during a meeting. Being able to clearly label a vague behaviour really help communicate expectations effectively.

Still, several people (and by that I mean friends that happens to be real accountants) suggested I change the terms to more politically correct versions: such as animal names or movie characters.

But if you read carefully this book you'll remember that I'm a Nanny myself, and to be consequent with my internal service provider personality profile, the names are probably not going to change anytime soon.

Not sure what's your personality profile yet? Take the test:

www.GreenElephantTeam.com/isp3

About the Author

Simon Chapleau is the founder of Green Elephant (www.GreenElephantTeam.com), a company that works with internal service providers around the world to help them deliver amazing value to their internal clients.

He won the Octas in 2010 for the enterprise project of the year, and he holds masters degree in project management, marketing and an MBA. He currently works hard to finish his doctorate with the Edinburgh Business School.

Simon regularly speaks at conferences around the world. He also delivers Green Elephant programs to private clients.

Prior to founding Green Elephant, Simon was CIO for Sanimax, a large North-American recycling company . He has also been involved in several business transformation projects with major clients such as Allstate, Procter and Gamble and ING as a director for Gartner, a leading IT management consulting firm.

Simon lives in Montreal with his wife and daughter.

Green Elephant

Green Elephant's clients range from public sector, insurance, large retailers and pharmaceutical companies. The company has expertise with internal service providers such as IT, HR and finance. Its services includes:

SPÄRK - Ignite your team. You team wants to provide amazing service, but how is it done? In this half-day workshop your team will understand the importance of satisfaction.

GRÖW - Creating amazing value. How do you find time to create amazing value when everyone is so busy with the day-to-day? In this program, we tackle the barriers that prevent your team from creating amazing value.

ALÏGN - All in one direction. Is your team aligned with the business? Don't guess, measure. ALÏGN can help you measure alignment scientifically.

PÜLS - Track user satisfaction. Do you know how satisfied your users are? With PÜLS you will get a monthly user satisfaction scorecard.

You can learn more at www.GreenElephantTeam.com

References

Part I.
- National Health and Social Life Survey (NHSLS) results of married and cohabiting couples' sexual activities,
- Hsieh, J.J.P. & Petter, S., 2012. Impact of user satisfaction with mandated CRM use on employee service quality. <u>MIS Quarterly</u>, 36(4), pp.1065–1080.
- User expectation and service performance - Szajna and Scamell (2001)
- McNulty, J.K. & Karney, B.R., 2004. Positive expectations in the early years of marriage: should couples expect the best or brace for the worst? Journal of personality and social psychology, 86(5), pp.729–43.
- Staples, D.S., Wong, I. & Seddon, P.B., 2002. Having expectations of information systems benefits that match received benefits: does it really matter? Information & Management, 40(2), pp.115–131.
- Oliver Richard L. and Swan John E., "Consumer Perceptions of Interpersonal Equity and Satisfaction in Transactions: A Field Survey Approach.", Journal of Marketing. 53 (April), 21-35 (1989)
- Andreasen, A.R., 1985. Consumer Responses to Dissatisfaction in Loose Monopolies. , 12(September), pp.135-142.
- Tarafdar, M., Tu, Q. & Ragu-Nathan, T.S., 2010. Impact of Technostress on End-User Satisfaction and Performance. Journal of Management Information Systems, 27(3), pp. 303-334.
- Jia, R. & Reich, B.H., 2011. IT Service Climate — An Essential Managerial Tool to Improve Client Satisfaction With IT Service Quality. *Information Systems*, pp.174–179.
- Amato, P.R., Loomis, L.S. & Booth, A., 1995. Parental Divorce, Marital Conflict, and Offspring Well-being during Early Adulthood. Social Forces , 73 (3), pp.895–915.

- Ferguson, J.L. & Johnston, W.J., 2011. Customer response to dissatisfaction: A synthesis of literature and conceptual framework. Industrial Marketing Management, 40(1), pp.118–127.
- McNulty, J.K. & Karney, B.R., 2004. Positive expectations in the early years of marriage: should couples expect the best or brace for the worst? Journal of personality and social psychology, 86(5), pp.729–43.
- Staples, D.S., Wong, I. & Seddon, P.B., 2002. Having expectations of information systems benefits that match received benefits: does it really matter? Information & Management, 40(2), pp.115–131.
- Burnham, T.C., 2006. Games: Ultimatum. In L. Nadel, ed. Encyclopedia of Cognitive Science. John Wiley & Sons, pp. 238–245.
- Ferguson, J.L. & Johnston, W.J., 2011. Customer response to dissatisfaction: A synthesis of literature and conceptual framework. Industrial Marketing Management, 40(1), pp.118–127.

Part II.
- Jia, R. & Reich, B.H., 2012. IT service climate, antecedents and IT service quality outcomes: Some initial evidence. The Journal of Strategic Information Systems.
- Bardhan, I.R. et al., 2010. An Interdisciplinary Perspective on IT Services Management and Service Science. Journal of Management Information Systems, 26(4), pp.13–64.
- Khaiata, M. & Zualkernan, I. a., 2009. A Simple Instrument to Measure IT-Business Alignment Maturity. Information Systems Management, 26(2), pp.138–152.
- Guillemette, M.G. & Paré, G., 2012. Toward a new theory of the contribution of the IT function in organizations. MIS Quarterly, 36(2), pp.529–551.

- Wiseman, R., 2003. Be lucky it's an easy skill to learn, Available at: http://www.telegraph.co.uk/technology/3304496/Be-lucky---its-an-easy-skill-to-learn.html.

Part III.
- Reyes, N.R. et al., 2012. Similarities and differences between weight loss maintainers and regainers: a qualitative analysis. Journal of the Academy of Nutrition and Dietetics, 112(4), pp. 499–505.
- Dagger, T.S., Danaher, P.J. & Gibbs, B.J., 2008. How Often Versus How Long. Journal of Service Research, 11(4), pp.371–388.
- Mogilner, C., Shiv, B. & Iyengar, S., 2012. Product choice: When are consumers most satisfied? Journal of Consumer Research.
- Ferguson, J.L. & Johnston, W.J., 2011. Customer response to dissatisfaction: A synthesis of literature and conceptual framework. Industrial Marketing Management, 40(1), pp.118–127.

www.ingramcontent.com/pod-product-compliance
Lightning Source LLC
Chambersburg PA
CBHW051446170526
45166CB00001B/139